AF215268

THE ELEPHANT AT THE DINNER TABLE

A JOURNEY INTO EXPERIENTIAL LEADERSHIP

AMIT NAGPAL

RUPA

Published by
Rupa Publications India Pvt. Ltd 2021
7/16, Ansari Road, Daryaganj
New Delhi 110002

Sales centres:
Bengaluru Chennai
Hyderabad Jaipur Kathmandu
Kolkata Mumbai Prayagraj

P-ISBN: 978-93-91256-30-2
E-ISBN: 978-93-91256-46-3

Sixth impression 2023

10 9 8 7 6

To my mother, Sudershan

The word 'sudershan' is derived from two Sanskrit words: 'su' (सु) meaning 'good' or 'auspicious' and 'darshan' (दर्शन) meaning 'vision'. Spiritual masters refer to it as the vision to understand the inner self.

Twenty-four hours before she left for her heavenly abode, on 29 June 2013, my mother advised me to:

- continue doing *sachha sauda*, which means 'to conduct business with truthfulness and integrity'
- focus on decluttering my life and my approach towards it
- emphasize on health and self-care

I dedicate this work to my mother, who ignited the spiritual side in me and encouraged me with the power of gratitude, service before self, faith, courage and perseverance. I hope I can live the next chapter of my life guided and inspired by her advice.

CONTENTS

FOREWORD

Tell me a fact, and I will learn. Tell me the truth, and I will believe. But tell me a story, share your experience and it will live in my heart forever.

—An ancient proverb

The world of work has changed dramatically over the past decade. Organizations are more global today and employee groups more diverse than ever before. Organizational structures are less hierarchical and more collaborative. And today's networked offices are full of technological distractions and an abundance of information that would have been unimaginable to the twentieth-century manager. With the COVID-19 pandemic, the way we define and describe the 'new normal' has changed radically too.

Today's learner is even more distracted, often untethered to a physical building, and overwhelmed by their responsibilities. In this new normal, almost 80 per cent of us find ourselves working from home and have vague and slim boundaries between professional and personal lives. Where does this leave time for training and development? Time spent on learning has been shoehorned into 24 minutes! Let us face it: working smarter, not harder, means finding ways to offer valuable training that employees can use (and that sticks for longer than a few minutes).

At the same time, many leaders and organizations who have embraced and promoted experiential learning have unique success stories.

I met Amit Nagpal in 1998, when I had recently joined as

the CEO of GE Capital International Services (GECIS), which would become India's largest and most successful Business Process Management (BPM) enterprise. After a successful transition of mortgage and collections processes from various GE organizations, my team was mandated to conceive and deploy our first healthcare business operation and transition some of the critical processes from GE Financial Services businesses in the United States.

We were looking for a leader with healthcare and training experience, and with a great appetite for learning new skills, someone who could seamlessly transfer knowledge within the shortest possible time and stabilize operations. Amit's profile fitted like a glove. His dedication to work, his insatiable thirst for knowledge, the ability to lead and inspire his team and reliable connects with the clients brought in quick results. Within a few months, Amit and his teams started generating revenue, saving millions of dollars for the client and expanding his work in managing healthcare claims, reinsurance processes and more.

In less than 18 months, his portfolio expanded from healthcare claims processing to reinsurance processes and, subsequently, to specialist processes of medical underwriting. He had a medical team driving quality and efficiencies that impressed our client's course, and delighted my executive team and me.

So, when Amit reached out to me to seek inputs on my leadership journey as a part of his book on experiential leadership, I was thrilled. I was more than happy to contribute my bit to honour Amit's two decades of contribution to the BPM industry. I wish and encourage him further in his pursuit of transforming learning and development. His firm's name Pursuitica, derived from three words: 'Pursuit', 'Curiosity' and 'Action', aptly describes Amit's journey as a self-made leader. He has much to share to aspiring leaders worldwide and can help make learning a big part of their lives.

After I finished reading the book, what struck me the most was Amit's sincere attempt to bring his stories, unique experiences and the associated learning to life. The writing style is simple, and the topic covered in each chapter is unique. Hence, one can pick up from any chapter at any given time, consume and relish it, and then go back to this buffet spread of exciting experiences and anecdotes.

The format is simple and flows well. Stories from Amit's experiences are fascinating and relatable. Commendable academic research, follow-through reflections journal and a curated list of resources for more in-depth insights and illustrations make this book an easy and joyful read.

Amit's selection of topics, triggered by his 31 years of diverse corporate journey, validated by years of painstaking research which included over 300 interviews, focused group discussions and surveys with leaders worldwide, make this work a compelling and deeply insightful read. Now I know and appreciate why it took him five years to conceive and deliver such an insightful book.

This book can most definitely be used as a work and resource material by leaders and management students, which is a huge bonus. I strongly suggest having a pen and paper or your recording device handy as this book is guaranteed to stimulate several moments of reflection and action plans.

While the book will inspire young aspiring leaders as well as first-time and mid-level leaders across all industries, there is enough to stimulate the senior leaders' minds too.

I hope you enjoy reading this book as much as I did. I hope it helps you with your quest in becoming a better leader and in making your career journey an impactful one.

Cheers!

28 October 2020

Raman Roy
Chairman and Managing Director,
Quatrro Global Services

INTRODUCTION

In my over 31 years of working with people professionally and otherwise, I have come in contact with leaders who have achieved an incredible amount of success. However, many of these leaders have found themselves struggling with an inner hunger, a deep need for congruence, healthy relationships and a purpose-driven life.

These struggles directly impact engagement levels with family and friends, employees, clients as well as other stakeholders.

Over the last five years, I have met over 300 leaders worldwide, who have represented leadership at all levels. During my interactions with them, the five most common refrains that I heard were about:

- The fear of not being good enough
- Unfulfilled potential
- Anxiety around the future
- The search for a purpose-driven career
- The inability to harmonize work and life

I have a feeling that some of these above problems may be familiar to you too. This book attempts to bring these conversations to the table to trigger ideas worthy of application at work and in life.

Thirty-three short stories based on my personal experiences will inspire you and invite you to the world of possibilities. By weaving my real-life experiences into academic research and a resource bank[1], I aim to make this an easy read as well as an enjoyable experience for my readers.

Grateful; Life is Awesome!
Amit Nagpal

---

[1]https://www.amit-nagpal.com/resources/, accessed 11 July 2021.

Leadership Research and Analysis

In the following pages, I have attempted to share a complete analysis of the 300 interviews with leaders worldwide, which became an essential input for discovering and validating this book's key themes. During the course of my research, I interviewed leaders across various age groups, with varying years of experience, and from diverse industries and global locations. Besides leaders from across the globe, several former colleagues, and management students from colleges such as the Symbiosis Institute of Management Studies, Pune and Xavier's University, Bhubaneshwar supported this research initiative in a big way.

My research specialist, Anneke van Aswegen, from South Africa, initially had no awareness of the Information Technology-enabled Services (ITeS) industry, especially in India. One of the main reasons for hiring a researcher from outside India was to make the analysis unbiased and objective. Key questions that we raised were around areas that the leaders wished to focus on in order to become more effective in their respective fields. We also discussed at length their struggles, challenges and key support areas. We split the data into three key segments: **team**

players (young leaders), **visionaries** (mid-level leaders) and **role models** (senior leaders). We shall discuss these three segments later in the chapter.

I wish to acknowledge the contribution of my research team members: Anneke, Mrinalini Sharma and Surbhi Sharma, and my illustration artist, Kasia Nowacka-Jakubowska.

A special mention goes to Anubha Mamgain, Tumpa Chatterjee, Vijay Colaco, Aseem Wadhwa, Neeti Khanka, Soumya Chakraborty, Manohar Garikapati, Pragati Bhargava, Sivakumaran Ranganathan, Malini Das Gupta, Prakriti Massey, Anshul Bhargava, Preeti Savio Freitas, Vikrant Bhatnagar, Reena Ravi, Pooja Srinivas, Vishal Ravikant, Melanie Moses, Sudhir Chaudhary, Amit Behki, Vivek Ghai, Sandhan D. Chowdhury and Brigadier Anant Nagendra.

I equally appreciate the rich and invaluable inputs received from Mrs Neelam Chakrabarty, the principal of India's top-ranked school, Delhi Public School, Pune.

Here, I would like to make a special mention of Raman Roy, a visionary who helped shape the $200 billion ITeS industry, worldwide. Raman is known as 'the Pioneer' and 'the father of the Business Process Management (BPM) industry' in India. Since 1992, he has played a pivotal role in promoting India as a preferred destination for Remote Processing to mainly North American and European organizations. He has directly created over 50,000 jobs in India and indirectly enabled over 800,000 people to support the BPM industry's creation through his pioneering efforts.

Raman is a pioneer four times over and has led Business Processing Outsourcing (BPO) initiatives of American Express, General Electric (now Genpact) and Spectramind (now Wipro BPM) before starting Quatrro in 2006. Under Raman's leadership, Quatrro grew to over 4,000 associates, serving more than 190 clients around the globe in almost eight years since its inception.

He has also played an active role in the ITeS industry's policy decision-making by working with the government on various initiatives. He served as Chairman of NASSCOM[2] in 2017.

I hope you will find the analysis shared in the following pages interesting and useful.

Leadership Research Findings

300 Leaders and Management Students across the globe

The Team Player (17–35 yrs)	The Visionary (25–44 yrs)	The Role Model (35–50 yrs)
Goals and desires		
• Earn respect and recognition • Attain financial freedom • Achieve excellence in the chosen domain • Be an industry expert • Win the trust of the team • Become a mentor • Be good at networking	• Be the best in the chosen domain • Deliver a TED Talk • Write and publish a book • Earn recognition for his value	• Head global operations • Create authentic leaders • Support his community • Do meaningful work • Make a difference

---

[2]NASSCOM (National Association of Software and Service Companies) is the industry association for India's IT and IT-enabled products and services sector.

The Team Player (17–35 yrs)	The Visionary (25–44 yrs)	The Role Model (35–50 yrs)
Pains and frustrations		
• Unclear customer requirements • Long working hours • Pressure to do more • Lack of direction and guidance • Lack of socializing skills • Having to deal with aggressive teammates • Fear of not being good enough	• Self-doubt • Unfulfilled potential • Lack of support at work • Bosses with prejudiced mindset • Office politics • Lack of recognition	• Stiff competition • Managing financial growth • Internal power struggle • Trying to build a talent pipeline of future leaders • Retaining employees
Learning aspirations		
• Business acumen • Self-awareness* • Managing change* • Big picture thinking skills* • Leadership readiness*	• Big picture thinking skills* • Leadership readiness* • Self-awareness* • Collaboration* • Global perspective • Cultural awareness	• Managing change* • Self-awareness* • Leadership readiness* • Collaboration* • Big picture thinking skills*

*Common learning requirements across all categories

For more details on this research, feel free to reach me at:

amit.nagpal@pursuitica.com

1

WHERE HAVE ALL THE LEADERS GONE?

I have travelled extensively throughout the world and discovered several great leaders in quite a few places; however, what struck me the most was the profound lack of authentic leadership in several areas. I feel honoured and excited when great leaders agree to share their experiences and wisdom with me.

Many people rise to the top in their profession, organization or department, company, and maybe, their community. But do they really know how to lead?

I have seen people in charge unable to make the right decisions and understand the people who report to them, are too overwhelmed by their responsibilities or are so involved in the process that they see only the trees but not the forest. They live on a project-to-project basis, neither advancing their organization's culture nor enriching lives of the employees in their care.

I guess I have a narrow view of leadership. But really, is it all that narrow? All I ask is the person in charge of a task or department should do justice to that appointment by taking the responsibility of bringing about a positive outcome in every area that comes under the ambit of that charge.

Good leadership entails going beyond project completion, reaching out to team members and giving them a significant say in the decision-making process. Good leadership also means taking chances, facing risk and the possibility of making mistakes (but learning from them), recognizing those who help and being honest with yourself and everyone else.

An authentic leader believes in the power of collective thought, someone who is confident enough to recognize that 'we are all in this together'. Leaders should have the ability to empower others so that they too can contribute to their particular strengths. Every person brings a certain skill set to the table, and this understanding gives leaders an edge.

As we embrace the post-COVID-19 world, empathy and trust will be two of the core drivers of successful leadership. Great leaders can develop strengths and become more effective. In recent years, the trend in employee reviews has been to acknowledge a strength or two and then focus on the person's weaknesses, often termed us 'improvement opportunities'. Why isn't the focus more on the person's strengths? Isn't that what made him a leader in the first place? It seems that leadership is strength-based and there is enough evidence of its seven to eight times impact on employee engagement levels. According to Bobby Chatterjee, Senior Director, HR, Hertz, there are some leaders who excel in a growth business while others excel in a period of decline or crisis situation. Only a small percentage appear to excel in both. Therefore, know yourself and be brave for the company's benefit. Step aside if the best leader for the next part of the journey is no longer you.

Leadership is part natural talent and part hard work. A leader may have a natural talent for innovation, but skill can only be honed and nurtured through awareness, practice and experience.

Now, I would like to tell you a story of leadership that drives home the point that you can accomplish whatever you set out to do. If you accept the challenge to become a better leader, you will achieve great things for yourself and help others do the same too.

The Beginning: An Ode to Raman Roy

The cave you fear to enter holds the treasure you seek.

—Joseph Campbell, American mythologist and writer

Nothing Is Impossible

Story #1

Circa 1995, John McDonald, a senior executive at American Express (Amex), visited India with his global leaders. He would often visit India as he saw 'human potential' here and hence this time, he chose New Delhi as the venue for his meeting. However, his leaders were not excited about India and started de-rating it by bringing up issues around poor infrastructure, poverty, etc. To humour them, John mentioned that an Indian Amex credit card customer owed money and that Raman Roy's team had repossessed his elephant as the customer was unable to pay his card outstanding!

After the meeting, John invited Raman over for drinks and dinner. John asked Raman to build on the story around the elephant.

The moment Raman greeted the leaders at the dinner table, they were all ears, mainly to confirm that John had indeed been pulling their leg at the meeting when he spoke about the elephant. There were many questions: How did Raman repossess this elephant when the customer was unable to pay the amount? Was Raman's team able to look after the animal? What did they feed him? These intriguing questions from the leaders triggered a bout of laughter at the table, as John watched Raman build on this story in sheer amusement.

Later that evening, John complimented Raman on the way he had managed to improvise the story so far and much to Raman's surprise, asked him to arrange for an elephant at the American Express office the next day. *'Has John lost his mind?'* Raman wondered. But he knew it must be a well-thought-out plan and so he excused himself from dinner to make a few calls to his team to make that happen.

Raman called his team and made this rather unusual request to organize for an elephant. It was late at night, and Raman further mentioned that since he was having dinner with the senior leaders, his team should leave a message at his home the moment they made arrangements to get an elephant.

By the time Raman reached home, it was pretty late. However, he chose to wake his wife up to inquire if there were any messages for him; he was clearly anxious. When Raman narrated the story, his wife, as expected, was equally surprised and asked Raman if he had lost his mind!

Raman could not sleep well that night and rushed to his office early in the morning to coordinate and brief his team on John's visit, which was scheduled in a few hours. Raman was assured by his team that they had hired an elephant from a place that rented out elephants for weddings and religious processions.

Since it was late in the night, it was challenging to get the elephant transported. Therefore, they decided to walk the elephant from downtown at 1 a.m. and was scheduled to reach the American Express office by 9 a.m. Raman briefed the entire team that they should have a context and that they conveyed a consistent message if asked about this elephant.

As John's entourage reached the office, he stepped out of his car and asked Raman if he had been able to arrange for an elephant. He was thrilled when Raman answered in the affirmative.

John was highly impressed with Raman's abilities to turn an idea into reality. The very fact that Raman was able to build on the story and organize an elephant in less than 12 hours, demonstrated his grit, confidence and ability to deliver. While John's team members were not very upbeat about the idea of outsourcing, Raman's interactions and actions convinced John and his team to give more work to Amex India.

In Raman's words, 'I believe this turned on a switch. They thought, "If these people want to do something, they can do it. They can get their act together if they put their mind to it." That, to me, was a turning point.'

Post this, John became quite close to Raman, and his idea called BPM, and he committed to multiple projects. As per Raman, many of these outsourcing projects were successful, while some were not. The efforts around making Amex India successful, and subsequently making GECIS successful paid off rich dividends. The success at GECIS inspired more BPM players to enter the Indian market. Raman's success at Spectramind in 2002 and subsequent acquisition of Spectramind by Wipro became a news headline. This prompted IBM to acquire Daksh eServices and Infosys+ Citibank to invest in Progeon, which later became Infosys BPO and subsequently, Infosys BPM. It has taken the Indian IT and BPM industry two decades to become a $200 billion industry and people like Raman sowed the initial seeds.

Raman demonstrated his capabilities around successfully and efficiently leading and managing the India back office. He demonstrated that a true leader:

- Is a visionary
- Takes risks
- Is innovative
- Is courageous
- Believes in their team and takes them along
- Displays a disposition of playfulness
- Is an inspiration

The elephant story became the talk of the industry, especially at American Express, GE and Spectramind. Raman's courageous and visionary move was around convincing the Amex leadership that India back office will help them save huge costs and will be more efficient. His abilities to hire and motivate his leadership team and a vision that this could be a revolutionary move for the organization and the country is well recognized and respected. The NASSCOM chairman position and several awards and recognitions validate it further. The GECIS success model created millions of opportunities for young graduates, support resources, technology specialists, leaders and people at the grass-root levels.

Had it not been for progressive politicians, bureaucrats and leaders, we as a nation wouldn't have been able to conceive and make this idea such a huge success. Today India is considered a leader in the BPM space.

Through this book, I would like to make a special mention of the leaders who have helped shape the Indian IT and ITeS industry. These leaders conceived new possibilities and took a leap of faith in the Indian workforce and in various government leaders. Collectively and individually, they shaped the industry and spread their wings across the globe.

Leaders such as the late Dewang Mehta (founder of NASSCOM), well-known telecom professional Sam Pitroda, N.R. Narayana Murthy (Infosys), Kiran Karnik (former president, NASSCOM), Mohandas Pai (Infosys BPM), Azim Premji (Wipro), Vineet Nayar (HCL), Keshav Murugesh (WNS), Natarajan Chandrasekaran (TCS), N.V. 'Tiger' Tyagarajan (Genpact), Ganesh Natarajan (Zensar), C.P. Gurnani (Tech Mahindra), Shiv Nadar (HCL) and Vikram Talwar (EXL) are truly worthy of special mention.

I firmly believe that everyone has the potential of a book in them. Life is a beautiful masterpiece bound together by our experiences. A day comes when your story wants to breathe on its own, have a life of its own. When people read it, they find a companion in their journey, they are assured that they are not alone. Isn't it interesting that our words (in a book) travel to places we have never been to? That has been one of the main motivations while writing this book.

My life has been full of new experiences, stories and informal learning. This book reflects on all the opportunities that came my way and how I took on multiple challenges, which sometimes led to success and sometimes to failures. At that stage, I never clubbed them as experiential learning. Now that I have completed 31 years in my corporate career, I felt this to be just the right time to reflect, compile and articulate my thoughts and share them with aspiring, young and mid-level leaders.

2

EMOTIONAL QUOTIENT: AT THE HEART OF LEADERSHIP

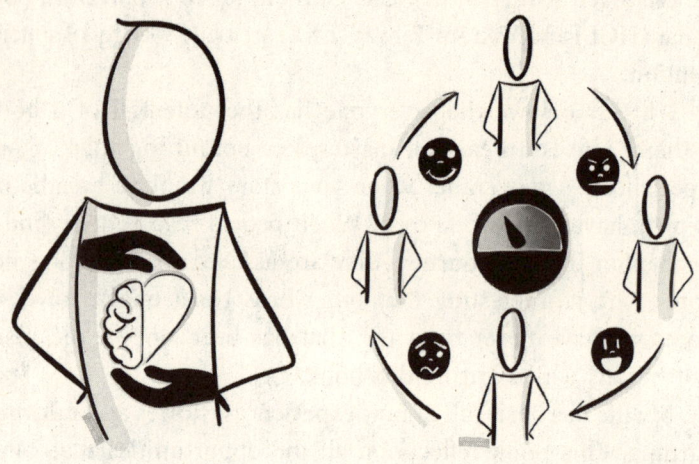

Emotional aptitude is a 'meta-ability', determining how well we can use whatever other skills we have, including raw intellect.

—Daniel Goleman, Author and science journalist

I am certain you must have heard of the term 'intelligence quotient' (or IQ as it is commonly known), which is the measurement of cognitive capabilities. IQ tests are standard in schools and other areas of academic pursuit. Another measure that has gained a lot of attention and application over the last decade is emotional intelligence or EQ—'the capacity to be aware of, control, and express one's emotions, and to handle interpersonal relationships judiciously and empathetically'.[1] Different dictionaries and think tanks offer various definitions and include different components of emotional intelligence which usually include self-awareness and self-regulation, motivation, empathy and social skills/relationship management. So, emotional IQ has to do with knowing and controlling yourself and playing well with others.

What I Learnt

Though the language and scope of emotional intelligence has entered the leadership space, many of us often wonder what emotions have to do with leadership. The short and simple answer to this question is: everything! According to the World Economic Forum, emotional intelligence is one of the top 10 skills needed to succeed in 2020 and beyond.[2] Many things are expected of you as a leader: you have to build consensus, know your people, foster trust in your teams, give direction and hold a vision. You also have to resolve conflicts and, in fact, it would be great if you could spot discontent brewing before it takes the shape of a full-fledged conflict. Leaders must have a finger on their team's pulse, the organization, the client's needs and moods as well as market realities. They must grow and develop themselves consistently as well. They cannot afford to rest on their laurels. That is a long to-do list, we all will agree. And yet, if you look at what underlines all these demands made of the leadership, it is the capacity to know oneself, gauge the other and impact people

[1]Goleman, Daniel, *Working with Emotional Intelligence*, Bantam, Reprint edition: 2000.
[2]Beckford, Avil, 'The Skills You Need to Succeed in 2020,' *Forbes*, 6 August 2018, https://www.forbes.com/sites/ellevate/2018/08/06/the-skills-you-need-to-succeed-in-2020/?sh=6f4397a6288a, accessed 28 June 2021.

and the environment around. It is still a tall order, but when we see the unifying aspects that form the core of good leadership, it becomes more manageable.

Here, let me share an example that showcases the importance of developing emotional intelligence in leaders. In 2008, when I rejoined Infosys to drive best practices in the Customer Services Centre of Excellence, I did not expect to be pulled into the thick of 'operations' as well. One of our telecom businesses was ramping up, yet, some of the key performance indicators (KPIs) were not being met. We were on a contract and it was clear that either we shape up or we ship out.

Baptism by Fire

Story #2

Swaminathan D. (Swami), our chief operating officer (COO) at that time, whom I was reporting to, asked whether I was willing to roll up my sleeves and jump in, even though this was over and above my profile. Life and business rarely come with a job description and, so, I said yes.

As you can imagine, this presented an awkward situation for my colleague, who was then managing the process. And, while the request was based purely on professional necessity, there was a personal and emotional aspect to it as well. My involvement created a sense of threat. I could sense the resistance to the fact that someone with similar experience and credentials was being brought on board to firefight. Most of the suggestions I made or the interventions I recommended were refuted or challenged. With a tight timeline and high stakes, I knew something had to change, else, we were headed towards failure.

I cannot say that I knew enough about emotional intelligence at the time to have decided my next steps. Still, somewhere, in my gut, I knew that we had to talk through this in a safe and mutually understanding environment to create the alignment and synergy required to bring this process to a successful closure. To build an environment of trust and commitment, I took the following steps:

- Aligned my work hours to map with the teams (i.e., night shifts for around five months)
- Rolled up my sleeves and participated in floor walks and observing calls (i.e., sidejacking)
- Spent time with high performers during breaks in capturing their best practices
- Participated in client calls, internal performance review meetings and vendor-manager interactions (formal and informal)
- Worked closely with the quality and training teams and shared some of their workloads

My colleague felt similarly happy, and through a series of closed-door conversations, where we aired our apprehensions and concerns, we were able to agree on presenting a unified face to the team. Such an action is not manipulation; a team needs to know that its leadership is pulling in the same direction. The leadership needs to create spaces where differences can be respectfully put out and a consensus reached.

While this may sound like a familiar story and the approach may seem commonsensical, we often forget that people must develop a range of internal skills to allow such conversations to bear fruit. Much 'dialogue and talking' occurs in personal and professional spaces without positive results.

It would be fair to say that we did have our own share of disappointments and heated exchanges, asking our leaders to help us by intervening as and when required. It took a churn to get to see clear waters. Having executive-level support from the chief executive officer (CEO) Amitabh Chaudhry's office helped. Moreover, the results were positive and within five to six months of sweat and toil, and the teams' tireless work, we delivered results and regained the client's confidence.

Emotional Intelligence and the Financial Bottom Line

Often, companies put emotional intelligence in the bracket of 'soft skills', which gives it a sort of 'step-cousin' treatment. Technical- and process-level skills become the 'hard skills' and the rest is seen as the icing that is good to have but not essential. Nothing could be further from the truth. There are numerous documented examples[3] of how people with a greater capacity to harness the power of their own emotions and connect with those of others have created 'real', tangible and financial value in their organizations.

According to a research paper titled *The Business Case for Emotional Intelligence* that was published on *Workforce. com*: 'restaurants managed by managers with high emotional intelligence showed an annual profit growth of 22 percent versus an annual average growth of 15 percent for the same period'.[4] Besides, people with high EQ scores make $29,000 more per year than their lower EQ counterparts.[5]

Teamwork Works!

Story #3

My own experience of handling the business operations for a UK-based telecom giant, BT, substantiates teamwork. My partnership with another colleague, Samir Pradhan, who led the project

---

[3]https://www.amit-nagpal.com/resources/, accessed 28 June 2021.
[4]Andrews, Shawn, 'The Business Case for Emotional Intelligence,' *Workforce. com*, 18 September 2018, https://www.workforce.com/news/the-business-case-for-emotional-intelligence, accessed 28 June 2021.
[5]Ibid.

management team, resulted in a seamless ramp up for our client from 90 employees to 1,100 in 13 months (by February 2006). We went through a series of difficult conversations. Some of these sparked emotional responses, but our cool-headed approach and transparency set a positive tone and gave a standard and calibrated view to the client as we went about scaling up on resources and infrastructure.

We were able to combine our strengths and share credit through timely and appropriate handling of multiple situations recognizing the many people who supported us simultaneously. My strong team of leaders, Sharad Choudhary and Smitta Kejriwal, and their focus on seamless operations and a rock-solid relationship with their client managers helped tremendously in ramping up in a short span. Regular weekly calls with the client, and being honest and upfront with them helped build mutual trust and understanding.

I have fond memories of Swami mentioning this noiseless and successful ramp-up in various discussions, including one with the organization's chairman, V. Balakrishnan.

At its core, I believe leadership is about instilling confidence in others.

—Howard Schultz, Former chairman and
CEO, Starbucks Coffee

◆

No doubt emotional intelligence is rarer than book smarts, but my experience says it is actually more important in the making of a leader. You just can't ignore it.

—Jack Welch, Former chairman and
CEO, General Electric

◆

Many of the vital attitudinal dispositions a leader needs to cultivate can be traced back to developing emotional intelligence. For example, I cannot imagine a leader being able to make an accurate self-assessment of strengths and drawbacks without creating a fair degree of self-awareness. Leaders who performed exceptionally well were mindful of their internal assumptions, reactions and motivations regarding external challenges, requirements and realities.

What Does the Practice of Emotional Intelligence Look Like?

For me, the most impactful way of focusing on developing emotional intelligence has been to consistently go back and become aware of the nature and impact of my behaviour on others. While a positive intention is a great starting point, one's behaviour is how it is perceived. Being in the moment, we are often unaware of how our words and actions are perceived by others. I try taking out a few minutes at the end of the day, or even *through* the day, to reflect on my thoughts. This exercise helps bring in a lot of clarity and calmness to the mind.

Being Honest About Mistakes

Story #4

It is essential to know your emotional triggers—things you feel strongly about, things that are likely to cause an outburst. Sometimes, even being aware of your stress levels can help you respond to situations in a calmer, more considered manner. This is learnt the hard way. In 1999, I was dealing with a challenging personal situation (someone in my family was diagnosed with cancer). One day, just as I was rushing across town to be with them, I learnt that someone in my team was not doing his job well. While addressing this situation, I could not separate the personal stress from the professional front, and I had an emotional outburst on the Operations floor. In fact, I have made similar mistakes twice or thrice in my career. My blaze caused this person a lot of embarrassment, and it made me a person I did not enjoy being. Thankfully, my manager understood, and I was able to apologize to this colleague and make amends.

Since then, I have been aware of situations where an 'emotional seepage' might occur, and I create an action plan to avoid it. Over the years, I have earned a healthy amount of goodwill amongst my colleagues and team. My colleagues saw my behaviour as an aberration brought on by my personal stresses rather than the norm. When such an understanding is possible, you create a cushion for instances where we react in unhelpful and sometimes destructive ways. This, of course, cannot be Plan A on how to handle emotions, but it does serve as a safety net at times.

The essential learning for a leader is to become comfortable with admitting one's mistakes and apologizing to make amends. This is something we all struggle with. Interestingly, an apology is not just a mumbled 'sorry'. It must be authentic and have the energy of your intention behind it. Else, it falls flat. And building safeguards to ensure the goof-up does not happen again is as essential as an acknowledgement. Hence, managing self becomes even more critical.

Before you lead others, you must first learn to manage yourself and become mature in reacting to the demands of the job. It is essential to learn how to treat success and failure with the same calm regard. Become resilient in the face of daunting change and challenge, become comfortable with moving priorities and treat others with compassion even when you have high expectations.

Learning about yourself, your attitudes, your emotions, your personality, your reactions, your ego and your fears—and their effect on others and on your managing effectiveness—is the experience you need at the start. Raising your EQ is a strong beginning.

The need to become emotional intelligence-sensitive can't be overemphasized, particularly in current times, when leaders' actions are being observed 24/7 even intruding their personal interactions at cinemas, airports, restaurants, public events and social events via social media platforms.

At GE, I got introduced to another concept of handling differences and finding solutions with colleagues experiencing stress or difficulties. The idea was simple and effective. Employees were encouraged to reach out to a colleague with whom they had an issue, offer a coffee meeting outside the office and discuss a way forward. As a rule, an offer for a 'workout' could not be declined. As a result, the organization found out that almost 90 per cent of the issues could be resolved with this simple initiative. Only a handful of such problems reached the seniors for intervention. I applied this method at GE and Infosys, and found it quite helpful.

Thus, leaders can help themselves by reflecting on their actions, thoughts and feelings throughout the day. One of my dear friends and fellow leadership consultants, Bobby Chatterjee, makes it a point to write at least 10 things she is grateful for, every evening before going to bed. Bobby has been practising it for the last several years. The exercise provides her with an opportunity for self-reflection and optimism from the positive experiences of the day. Inspired by Bobby, I too have started writing five lines every morning, reflecting on the previous day and trust me, it is quite healing and helpful.

At Wipro, during a talk to the newly appointed senior leadership, I had the excellent opportunity to hear Azim Premji, the former chairman of Wipro Technologies. He made it a point to be in his office at least 30 minutes prior to getting involved in the routine work, and utilize this uninterrupted early morning time to reflect on his goals and make notes on his plans for the day and beyond. His secretary was instructed not to disturb him during this period.

Developing the capacity to be objective while managing highly stressful situations becomes critical as you grow as a leader and as your responsibilities multiply. Practising this skill early on gives you an edge over others. However, our personal reflections need to be supplemented by perspectives and inputs from others. No matter how well we see ourselves, there is always something we miss out on. And, in so many ways, it is about how people perceive you. Whenever young leaders or even experienced ones find themselves struggling with receiving feedback or having an accurate perception of themselves or their team, it is a good idea to invite inputs from those you trust to get perspective and clarity.

In the new economy, there are so many moving parts that one leader cannot possibly keep an eye on all the balls in the air. The definition of success has broadened from looking at individuals to managing teams. In this context, young leaders need to be open about their struggles and challenges. Developing and nurturing a circle of people whose advice you can rely on is crucial. Believing that you know it all or can do it all is a sure path to failure. Work on developing secure bases[6] that will allow you to raise valid question. The quest is essential in this world.

Aside: I have benefited immensely by hiring a coach while working at Infosys. I wish I had taken this decision much earlier in my career.

Quest for Emotional Intelligence

The word 'quest' is an important one for leaders to keep their eye on. Often, there is a belief amongst leaders and organizations

---

[6]Kohlreiser, George, *Hostage at the Table: How Leaders Can Overcome Conflict, Influence Others and Raise Performance* (John Wiley and Sons: 2011).

that emotional intelligence can be 'learnt' or 'acquired' during a workshop. And while workshops and learning spaces are great starting points to begin exploring our own awareness level, that is not the endpoint. Developing greater self-awareness and the capacity to regulate emotions, positively impact others, etc., is an ongoing journey where the signposts are internal. There is no framework or matrix against which to compare yourself. This is not a place you arrive at, or *stay* either. With changing circumstances and contexts, your capacity to be aware too will change.

Recognizing that it is normal and human to make mistakes or misjudge a person or situation, is essential. Often, young leaders are tough on themselves and strive to *never make a mistake.* Ironically enough, what is required is an action plan on how to *deal with* blind spots. How to apologize well, how to course correct quickly—these are the skills that need development.

People often say, strike a balance between being too lenient and too autocratic; too hurried and not quick enough; micromanaging and not being available enough! Finding the balance might seem like a challenging task. Often, we look for external indicators such as people's reactions and inputs. These can be useful guides, but not in all situations. Then there are internal indicators, such as our own gut instinct and inner voice, which can serve as a rudder to show us the direction. Once you have spent time tuning into that part of yourself, you know where *your* balance lies. Once you are sure, even when you are swimming against the tide, you *know,* and you stay the course. That is what investing in developing your emotional intelligence does.

On this subject, Sam Swaminathan, a senior performance consultant and a great friend, mentions that, while the performance metric is important, not everything needs to be measured. If the celebrated tennis player Roger Federer had only focused on the scoreboard and not on the game, he would not have reached the pinnacle to stand among the most legendary tennis players. The metric is an outcome. The world is not black and white but grey, and many shades of grey. We must learn to navigate through the different shades, and hence, having a balanced emotional view and objectivity serves well during our leadership journey.

While most of us are self-aware, self-regulation takes more importance in our lives. For example, while we may be aware that we are impatient (self-awareness), what are we doing about it (self-regulation)? Many of us are guilty of not being able to regulate our emotions. When you surround yourself with people who are better than you, the rub-off is positive. Sam considers his better half as an emotionally intelligent person and applies some of her advice, especially on matters where you decide to support/forgive the other person even when you have the power to say no.

Emotional Intelligence in the Personal Space

Two events in my life have triggered profound moments of reflection. The first being my mother's death in 2013 and the other a five-month Co-Active coaching journey with the Coach Training Institute (CTI) in 2017–18. These events have been unique tipping points and have helped me understand and appreciate emotional intelligence better.

My mother always stressed upon the benefits of following an uncomplicated and uncluttered life. She embodied the impeccable integrity, spirituality and values of a Servant Leader. On top of it, till her last breath, she practised what she preached. CTI training further added a profound and deep impact on a professional and personal front.

Here are some learning nuggets from my Co-Active Coaching journey:

- Seek answers from within
- Find a captain/North Star to guide you (i.e., mentor or leader whom you can reach out to for unconditional

support and guidance)
- Know that you have all the power to fight your inner gremlins
- Understand the need and benefits of being non-judgmental
- Learn the power of active listening skills
- Communicate succinctly and bottom-line your conversations

Considering these points further, aren't these integral and essential components of an emotionally intelligent and resilient leader?

Here is another interesting anecdote to further explain the application of emotional intelligence in real life.

A True Leader Engages Back

Story #5

In 2006, I joined as Operations Leader at Infosys, managing a large telecom giant and reporting to Swaminathan (Swami), who was then the head of the telecom business vertical. My initial observations on Swami were around his being number-oriented and direct, and a results-focused leader. He was based out of the company headquarters in Bangalore (now Bengaluru), and I was based in Pune. Swami also believed in delegating, and so we had limited phone calls, reviews and occasional personal meetings in Pune or Bangalore. Irrespective of the limited interaction, I kept him posted regularly via emails and text messages, including news of achieving certain milestones and birthdays of my team.

To my disappointment, I would rarely see Swami writing or calling this colleague to wish them on their birthdays, anniversaries, etc. This further reinforced my image of him as someone who was purely business centric. However, this interpretation took a 180-degree turn a few months later. This was the time when I had put in my papers to join Cognizant as their Business Head for Healthcare. One day, I received a call from Swami asking me to join him and the larger telecom team for a business off-site. I tried to politely decline by saying that it would be inappropriate for me to join a strategy meeting during my notice period. However, Swami insisted, and I had no option but to initiate my travel and be present at the off-site. On the closing date, Swami invited me to the stage to announce my decision to leave Infosys. His voice still echoes in my mind; he mentioned the excellent work I had done over the last one-and-a-half years and how I would be missed. The absolute stunner was when he said, and I quote, 'The doors of Infosys are always open for you whenever you decide to come back.'

This gesture left me teary-eyed and with a realization of Swami's emotional dimension.

My tenure at Cognizant was short-lived. This was primarily because of the change of organization strategy to move the majority of healthcare projects to the Chennai headquarters. It was a challenge to relocate with my family, mainly because of our newly born daughter. I continued to long to return to Infosys with an affirmation of the respect and the open offer from a senior executive.

During a chance meeting with Swami at a NASSCOM conference in Bangalore, I decided to encash the offer to return. Swami appreciated my need to take on a more cerebral and global role.

Since then, my perceptions and perhaps my unconscious bias were challenged and shot down. I further realized that each person has a unique way of expressing themselves. I continue to admire Swami's leadership. He continued to mentor and encourage me to take up multiple assignments and challenges in my second stint that lasted more than eight years.

To many of us, this may sound too good to be true. I have struggled while applying some of the concepts, and the journey of self-discovery continues to date. My relationship with my 24-year-old son can be considered as one example of the struggles. Often, we fall into the trap of confusing coaching with counselling and mentoring. To add to it, as a protective parent, I have crossed a line several times and sounded preachy and solution-centric. Both of us, being strong personalities, have been defensive, shown a lack of empathy and, more importantly, reacted with poor listening abilities.

However, having now become a lot more aware of emotional intelligence concepts, I have been able to reflect deeper, have sought help and support from a fellow CTI coach, Siat Yeow, and found answers that seem to be working well for both of us. I am glad to share that our conversations have now become more meaningful and engaging.

Therefore, being aware is not enough. You need to practise the concepts, seek help and continue to act. A Growth Mindset is essential to develop our emotional intelligence (such as flexibility, or stress and uncertainty management) or leadership skills (finding ways to lead and motivate our team remotely) or to adapt to new technologies (learning how to use tools for remote working). The Growth Mindset works best when adapting to a new reality that may emerge after a crisis. I know of many people who try to reconstruct the past and continue to stay fixed in past habits.

Diving Deep: Research Insights

What is required of a person to create positive interaction spaces? I believe that creating spaces is the bedrock of successful teams and leaders. Daniel Goleman, the EQ visionary, has written at length about emotional intelligence, and I like his framework. Those who are not inclined to read through his several books (which I recommend wholeheartedly), a few articles[7] that sum up his ideas and findings, with recommendations on implementing them, should at least be read without fail. Reading them provides a good starting point to develop one's emotional intelligence. Briefly, emotional intelligence is not about 'controlling' or 'not expressing' emotions. Instead, it is about the following five aspects.

1. Self-awareness: It is the capacity to *recognize* what you are feeling and what is *causing* that feeling to occur.
2. Self-regulation: This is not an iron-like control over your feelings. Instead, it is the capacity to *manage* the emotions you are experiencing and then deciding with the help of your *thinking* mind how you would like to respond[8] to the events that triggered those feelings in you.

   This could very well be the most misunderstood of the five aspects of emotional intelligence. It does not speak of *control* in the traditional sense, but talks about modulating your expression of emotions. When people do that, they create an environment of trust and fairness. Politics and infighting, which can be the bane of any organization, get

---

[7]Goleman, Daniel, 'What Makes a Leader?' *Harvard Business Review,* January 2004, https://hbr.org/2004/01/what-makes-a-leader, accessed 28 June 2021.

[8]Viktor Frankl in his book titled *Man's Search for Meaning* (Simon & Schuster: 1984) beautifully demonstrates the difference between reacting and responding. He says that our true freedom lies in the moment between stimulus and response. He was able to practise this way of thinking in a Nazi concentration camp where he spent three years and experienced the loss of his entire family. I wonder how leadership in all areas of life would be transformed if we could take a page out of his book.

drastically reduced, while productivity increases. People want to join such organizations, and talented people are not tempted to leave. Emotional states are also contagious, and a calm boss will model an approach that many will organically adopt. The emotional state of leaders sets the tone for the organization.

3. Self-motivation: It is the capacity to tolerate setbacks and motivate yourself to move ahead. Resilience and perseverance are competencies that are built in the zone of self-motivation.

4. Social awareness: It is the capacity to clue into and be aware of the emotions of those around you. We exist in social contexts and define ourselves through our relationships. An ability to be mindful of the undercurrents of feeling around us is an essential aspect of emotional intelligence.

5. Empathy: This is a critical aspect of emotional intelligence that is required of leaders. The capacity to set boundaries considerately and command respect often stems from empathizing with others' experiences. There is no emotional capacity that is more misunderstood than empathy! People often confuse it with mollycoddling or an inability to say no. Nothing could be further from the truth.

Travis Bradberry and Jean Greaves identified another critical element in their book, *Emotional Intelligence 2.0*.[9] They call it 'relationship management'. Understanding your own behaviour and those of others around you enables you to build stronger relationships with the important people in your life. While the framework can be read and understood, the road to developing emotional intelligence is very much practise-driven. Just like you cannot learn to drive a car by reading about it in a manual, you

---

[9]Bradberry, Travis and Jean Greaves, *Emotional Intelligence 2.0*, Perseus Books Group, 2009.

cannot build your emotional capacities by simply reading a book.

Emotional Intelligence in Action

Story #6

I vividly recall my first visit to the US in 1998, with a team of four professionals that included two female and two male colleagues. For all of us, it was the first visit to that country; also, we had all joined the organization, GECIS, around the same time. For me, since it was a case of travelling within two weeks of joining, I had little interaction with my team. We had just reached our apartment in Orlando, Florida, after a long and tiring 24-hour journey. While I got to know about some difference-of-opinion-triggered conversation between the two lady colleagues during the flight, little did I know that it had reached a boiling point on our arrival to a new country!

I somehow mustered the courage to offer them a ride to the nearest restaurant to help them get a neutral environment, comforting food and, maybe, a bit of guidance from my end. The reason I mention 'courage' is that not only was this my first time addressing such a challenge before the initiation of our three-month project, but this was also the first time I drove a rental car in a right-hand driving country, and with no GPS! Soon, I realized that the warring colleagues were open to a dialogue, and an offer to step out for a quick meal helped them air their issues and seek an amicable way forward.

Over the next few weeks of living and working together, I was able to better understand and appreciate the anxieties around a new role, new country and new work environment. Spending quality time during breaks at work, informal interactions over dinner, sharing responsibilities, being open to talking about our challenges around the new role, and allowing private time and space to each other made a huge difference. I have fond memories of the successful project and all the fun we had during our off-time and weekends. We created incredible memories for ourselves and, to date, continue to cherish the camaraderie.

As I reflect on this experience, I am pretty convinced of emotional intelligence in action.

Emotional Intelligence vs Emotional Literacy

Claude Steiner's work *Emotional Literacy: Intelligence with a Heart*[10] is a gem in the plethora of Transactional Analysis writing. For those who wish to not just approach the *intelligence* aspect of emotional intelligence but also want to get a window into a more meaningful, holistic way of thinking about emotional intelligence itself, the book is available free of charge and can be downloaded from the Internet.

In his book, Steiner talks about how emotional intelligence alone could be used to manipulate as well. I have seen people

---

[10]Steiner, Claude, *Emotional Literacy; Intelligence with a Heart*, https://dgek.de/wp-content/uploads/2015/09/Steiner-Emotional-Literacy.pdf, accessed 28 June 2021.

use knowledge of these areas in ways that do not always create win-win situations. Steiner talks about how both Adolf Hitler and Mother Teresa could have high emotional intelligence; however, their intention and actions spoke to the presence or absence of emotional literacy.[11]

A colleague of my academic researcher Mrinalini Sharma, reported her friend's story, where she went into a meeting with her boss, a director, who appeared very caring and supportive. She asked for her involvement in a new project. The colleague came out of the meeting saying, 'I agreed to everything she said. Why did I do that? I really didn't want to do what she asked.' This was a form of manipulation disguised in the cloak of 'motivation'. It was a technique designed to benefit the director. But manipulation never works for exceedingly long. This director was released in less than six months on the job.

We do not often talk about 'heart' in the context of leadership, but more recently, the focus on leading with care and stewardship

---

[11]Ibid.: 31.

has gained popularity. Words such as 'heart', 'values' and 'integrity' need to become the mainstay of leadership training and only then will young leaders who begin their journey have much to look forward to.

The Jeff Bezos Story

As one of the richest men globally, Amazon founder Jeff Bezos's net worth is larger than some countries' gross domestic products (GDPs)—combined! What does the Amazon founder view as the top sign of intelligence? It's not money or prestige but the ability to admit when you are wrong.[12]

Emotional intelligence is the foundation of Bezos's strong leadership, and the primary reason for both his and the company's success. He leads in a way that recognizes and celebrates the softer sides of the business and puts him in charge of his emotions.

Here are three of the many ways Bezos demonstrates emotional intelligence:

1. He acknowledges challenges: Leaders are humans, not robots. They have emotions and understand that their employees have feelings as well. Instead of glossing over challenges, Bezos acknowledges them and their impact on his employees. One recent example came from his announcement of Amazon's response to the coronavirus pandemic. He began by acknowledging, 'These aren't normal circumstances'.[13] Acknowledging difficulties opens leaders up to empathy and making real, authentic connections with their teams. Successful companies aren't

---

[12]https://www.linkedin.com/pulse/3-ways-jeff-bezos-shows-emotional-intelligence-jacob-morgan/, accessed 10 July 2021.

[13]Bariso, Justin, 'A 4-Word Lesson in Emotional Intelligence from Jeff Bezos', *Inc.com,* https://www.inc.com/justin-bariso/a-4-word-lesson-in-emotional-intelligence-from-jeff-bezos.html, accessed 28 June 2021.

immune to trials, but glossing over challenges can force leaders and employees to hide their emotions.

2. He is on even keel: Bezos faces constant scrutiny in his personal and professional life. It's a trend that many CEOs believe will continue to grow for future leaders. But even with massive amounts of criticism and public scrutiny, Bezos stays steady. He doesn't get riled up or snap at critics. He keeps his emotions in check to remain professional and courteous. That doesn't mean he can't be bold and passionate, but he does it in a way that protects him and his company. When claims of Amazon's allegedly callous workplace practices topped the news,[14] Bezos didn't fire back. Instead, he defended Amazon's culture and encouraged employees who had faced issues to contact the HR or to email him directly. His direct response showed his passion without taking away from the seriousness of the case.

3. He surrounds himself with more intelligent people: A cornerstone of emotional intelligence is self-awareness or knowing your own strengths and weaknesses. Bezos is aware of the fact that he doesn't have the answer to every problem, so he intentionally builds teams with more intelligent or more experienced people than him. That self-awareness and humility allows him to follow his own advice and admit when he doesn't know the answer.

The Elon Musk Example

In one of its articles, *Inc.com* describes Elon Musk as a man of extraordinary genius and vision.[15] Musk is said to be amiable

---

[14]https://www.linkedin.com/pulse/3-ways-jeff-bezos-shows-emotional-intelligence-jacob-morgan/, accessed 10 July 2021.
[15]Boitnott, John, 'The Power of Emotional Intelligence Is on Full Display

and media-ready. He is charming and articulate, with a bit of showmanship thrown in. In response to a recent claim that Tesla had incurred 30 per cent more employee injuries than the industry standard, Musk committed to personal accountability in an email to employees. He indicates that it broke his heart whenever an employee was injured while building cars, and that he sincerely cares for the well-being and safety of his people.

He then asked to be notified directly about every injury, to meet with the injured employees personally and attempt to do their tasks, so that he could understand what needed to be fixed.

'This is what all managers at Tesla should do as a matter of course. At Tesla, we lead from the front line, not from some safe and comfortable ivory tower. Managers must always put their team's safety above their own.'[16]

Emotional intelligence characterizes the most admirable of human organizations. And, some of the world's best leaders use emotional intelligence that expands their businesses.

---

with Elon Musk, Jeff Bezos, and Ursula Burns,' *Inc.com*, https://www.inc.com/john-boitnott/3-ceos-who-are-using-emotional-intelligence-to-expand-their-business.html, accessed 28 June 2021.
[16]Ibid.

It is very important to understand that emotional intelligence is not the opposite of intelligence, it is not the triumph of heart overhead—it is the unique intersection of both.

—David Caruso, American actor and producer

◆

Empathy is simply listening, holding space, withholding judgment, emotionally connecting, and communicating that incredibly healing message of you're not alone.

—Brené Brown, Author

For You to Reflect in Your Own Light

This section is for you to reflect on what you have read this far. What key messages have stayed with you from the chapter?

_____

_____

_____

_____

_____

_____

Having an emotional seepage is normal and makes us human. However, seepages that do not serve us well, if left unattended can harm us. Seepages come in many forms, for example, having a breakdown in front of your colleagues. Another example could be getting into a heated argument with someone on the road, anything that throws you off balance.

Here's a short exercise:

Write down what your emotional seepages at work look like. (You can repeat this exercise for home as well.)

_____

_____

_____

_____

_____

Create a personalized early warning system. Stay with this awareness. Next time it happens, try slowing down deliberately. The alarm in your head will ring and tell you, 'YOU are doing this again!'

Create an Action Step that can help you stop the next time. List it here.

For example, keep a funny reminder in the form of a poster that tells you shouting doesn't help or taking a short walk before responding to an unpleasant situation or person. You could also plan a coffee break. Think of the person you are having difficulties with. Offer them a cup of coffee or a meal in a neutral environment. Display your sincere intent to resolve issues amicably.

_____

_____

_____

_____

_____

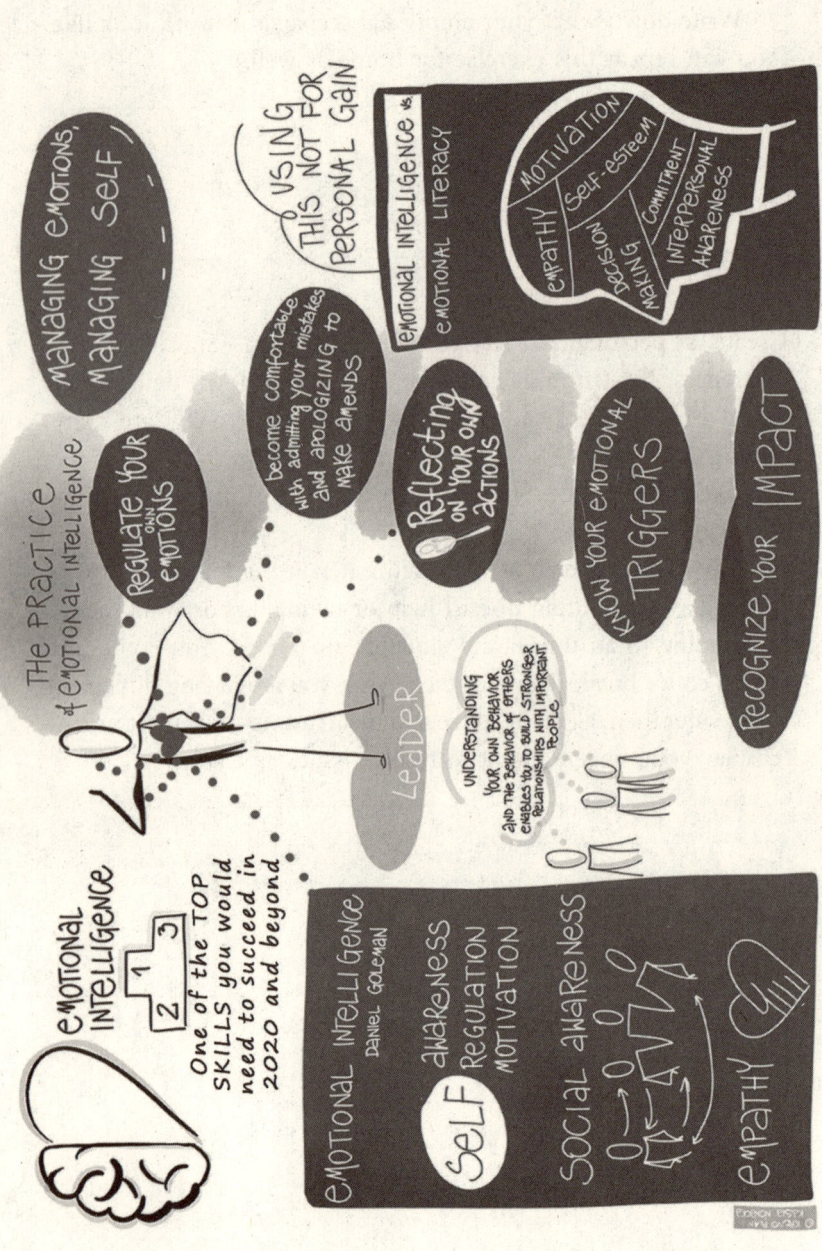

3

FIND A MENTOR TO GUIDE YOU

I'm always ready to learn, although I don't always like being taught.

—Winston Churchill,
Former British prime minister

Experiential learning is all about learning by doing. The first thing to do is improve your self-awareness and self-regulation to control yourself and, to whatever extent possible, the reactions and thoughts of those around you.

There is a saying that you cannot take the splinter out of someone else's eye if you have a bigger one in your own. Self-management is a requisite discipline if you are to lead others.

Now, a leader does need emotional intelligence to be resilient, honest and transparent. But what if you need some help with understanding yourself and how you are affecting others? Making a critical mistake in management can lead to organizational downfall. You may want to improve your decision-making and behaviour modelling, but wouldn't it be great if you had someone to advise you? Wouldn't it be great if you could approach a senior member of your organization—a seasoned manager, a tenured professor, an acclaimed doctor, a senior partner?

We could also connect with some other experienced person who might be interested and capable of guiding you through those rough waters. Finding the right person to mentor might be a challenge, but it is definitely worth the search. Finding someone highly qualified in your field, well respected in your organization and willing to offer you assistance and guidance can be one of the most critical actions you can take to be a successful leader. And it is a step often overlooked by many aspiring leaders.

Mentoring is not limited to your professional life alone. Family, friends and acquaintances can also be of immense help in your understanding of yourself and how you are growing and influencing others. The path to leadership can start at any time, even when you are young and learning to model the behaviours of people you admire.

What I Learnt

Curiosity and Asking for Help Work

Story #7

I have been lucky to have had multiple people in my life who modelled different behaviours, and I am grateful that I had the openness to take in and learn from them. Even during my childhood in Agra, I remember being moved by my neighbour Sonali Chandra's kindness and generosity. After Dad passed away, our family was struggling to make ends meet. She was so courteous and knew the troubles we were facing. Often, she would come to the back door of our home with a portion of meat that she had cooked for her family and saved especially for me. She saw that I was both working and studying, and wanted to make sure that I ate well. In fact, she taught me how to eat correctly—the right food, in the correct manner. Her husband worked at Bata and she ensured I was never without a good pair of shoes. Her unbridled generosity and thoughtfulness taught me to look out for those around me and be grateful for the unexpected kindnesses people bring into our lives.

Even my early start in mastering the English language is attributed to her. She would take me to English movies and correct my pronunciation. I would say 'ammution' for 'ammunition', and she would fix that. I was also the lucky sole beneficiary of her subscriptions to magazines such as *National Geographic, Reader's Digest* and *India Today*. I was the only one allowed to take these resources back home, as she knew that I would take good care and return them in good condition. Her gesture widened my horizons and encouraged a love of learning that has continued to stay with me. I would share with her my academic journey, and she would often point the way forward. As a child, I found her inputs and guidance invaluable for my development, and she left a profound and indelible mark on my life.

In my early years, another vital role model was Stanley Dharamsevak, my economics teacher during high-school days. A handsome man, he wore suits to class, had an excellent command over English and a flair for teaching economics. His presence and capacity to simplify complex ideas impacted me immensely. I continue to be inspired by him as I make changes in my delivery style and stories while connecting with different audiences. During our recent school alumni meet, we invited Mr Dharamsevak to grace the event, and since then, I have been in regular touch with him.

Several other leaders have left a lasting impression on me. However, identifying one amongst many such leaders is a difficult task. Some of their unique leadership styles and approaches have significantly impacted my career over the years.

Some of the typical traits that I saw in most of the leaders who have influenced me are:

- People centricity
- Detail orientation
- Excellence in communication and oration
- Process improvement orientation
- Objectivity, and feedback- and data-centric
- Confidence
- Solution orientation

Objectivity in Action!

Story #8

Upendra Singh, the leader who used to head Operations during my stint at Spectramind, was conducting a performance review with all his directs when the phone rang. It was Upendra's daughter, who was seeking his permission on some issue and he kept turning her down. He mentioned that he had already discussed the matter with her in detail, and that there was no scope of revisiting. We all felt a little uncomfortable and wanted to excuse ourselves out of the father–daughter discussion. However, Upendra gestured us to remain seated.

Finally, after some time, the personal discussion came to an end, with Upendra sticking to his original point of not revisiting the topic. The entire conversation was made with no raised voice or change in temperament. He maintained a strict professional approach, apologized for the interruption and continued with his review. My take on this is that our leader meant business and conveyed a clear message to all of us on his no-nonsense approach while dealing with both personal and work issues.

Gopal Devanahalli, my former leader at Infosys, is great at multitasking. He would ask me questions on what book I am reading currently as we got to meet at airports, coffee areas, etc. Swaminathan, my former leader at Infosys, helped me learn the importance of maintaining a diary, switching gears from a severe meeting to a lighter conversation with another group.

Keeping the Balance

Story #9

Anju Talwar, my leader at GE, is a classic example of someone who tactfully manages a work-life balance. I vividly recall that in the early year of setting up a business at GECIS, we went for a leased office space. In 1998, the cost per seat was ₹30,000 ($600) per month, and hence, it was a no brainer to share office seats, primarily since many of us used to manage work during night shifts. I was one of them and would share Anju's office seat. I would patiently wait for her to end her day, and since we had an open seating plan, I was able to overhear most of her conversations.

One conversation that I recall very well is of Anju giving instructions to her cook over a speakerphone, asking if her husband was back from work, and if her son had finished his dinner. She would gracefully handle both work- and home-related pressures and never lost her cool. Always available to her teams, extremely objective, data-driven and a solution-centric professional, Anju was someone I looked up to. This was a leader who was clearly way ahead of her times and never sought any special considerations and worked her way up to become a senior executive vice president and set up several centres in China and other global locations.

Key learning from my leaders and clients:

- *Your work speaks for you. Intense focus on bottom lining conversations.*
  Rahul Dixit, my leader at GE, is a man of few words who is fair and data-driven. He stood up for his team.
- *Wisdom, maturity and being highly respectful*
  Stuart Hastings, Client (Friends Provident Insurance).
- *Data centricity, clear objectives; focus on results and quick response*
  Daniel Wixon, Client (Dell Computers)
- *Open and direct communication*
  Ian Fletcher, Client (British Telecom)
- *Hard work pays off*
  N.K. Seth, SC Arora (My leaders at GlaxoSmithKline)
- *Razor-sharp focus on action, energy and results*
  T.K. Kurian (Former CEO Wipro BPM and Wipro Ltd)
- *Active listening, great articulation and excellent vocabulary*
  Raghu (Raghavendra K, my former Leader at Infosys BPM)
- *Healthy people connect and timely recognition*
  Raman Roy

In my discussions with Gopal Devanahalli, he mentioned how he immensely gained from his leaders while at Infosys. He shared how much he learnt from Nandan Nilekani, co-founder, Infosys, about creating business value and understanding the client industry. Gopal continued to mention his learning on attention to detail, and a structured and robust approach from Amitabh Chaudhry, the then CEO of Infosys BPM. From Swami, Gopal learnt about client engagement and troubleshooting. Swami's ability to get into minute details and deep levels of client engagement has been beneficial.

Mentorship: Giving Fish to Eat?

Story #10

During my interview with Raman, he fondly remembered his mentor, Vinod Mehta.

Right from his early days in accountancy, one of the professionals who taught Raman the most was Vinod. He was the principal under whom Raman had done his apprenticeship for accountancy. Raman learnt a lot from him. In Raman's words, the concept in accountancy was that 'an accountant would understand the scrutiny of a ledger'. Vinod was a magician with ledgers. He would just open an accounts ledger (these were 120-page long) and put his finger on an error, almost effortlessly. They would sit there and be amused at his skill. Vinod would say, 'The numbers talk to me. Raman, you got to understand how the process works.'

Raman still has this ledger (ledger #4) from a client he was working for. He remembers that he had written his comments in that ledger, and when Vinod came to review it, he looked at the review and said in his vernacular, which translates thus: 'You can do it, I don't have to do it anymore.' It was a proud moment for Raman. He learnt a great deal by following Vinod. Vinod taught Raman everything step by step, and that was his experience of learning by following. Under a chartered accountant (CA), the entire apprenticeship concept is that your principal teaches you; you learn by observing.

But there is a flip side to it as well. Many of Raman's bosses taught him what not to do as well. Raman used to sit there as an employee and watch them as they took those decisions and treated their employees in a certain way. Raman used to turn around and say to himself, 'This is wrong.' So, you learn what to do and what not to do when you follow the lead of those around you. And a more significant part of Raman's learning has been what not to do rather than what to do.

Raman recalled another exciting incident with his guru, Vinod, during his CA days. 'There were four of us who came back from a vital audit to the office that day. For this audit, various people were leading other teams for different locations of the client. When we came to the office, Vinod asked us to sit and write the draft report and so we did just that.

'When he read my report, he blasted me. He asked me to rewrite it. The second guy was also given a similar feedback, but in his case, Vinod called his steno typist and dictated the report. He was assigned another audit, and he left. We were frustrated; we did not want to be in office because of restrictions.

'Vinod called me in the second time, read my report and rejected it again. I spent 10 extra days in office during this incident, rewriting the entire report. When I went to him the last time, he finally gave a green signal to get it typed. I asked him about the treatment I received; others were helped by dictating the report but not me. He smiled and replied, "You are capable of writing your own report. You are now giving your report to the typist to type; others were not capable." In those 10 days, I learnt a great deal about writing a report; he taught me everything by rewriting it several times. He is no more with us, but I am forever grateful to him for the learning I received.'

Mentorship is not about fishing for your employees and giving them the fish to eat. It is about identifying people who can do it and taking them through the learning, thus helping them do it. It is about teaching them how to fish for themselves.

Diving Deep: Research Insights

The Killer Elephants

Mrinalini, my academic research colleague, once narrated an intriguing story. It was about a herd of elephants that had gone rogue after being moved out of the Kruger National Park in the late 1990s.[17] Too large an elephant population had compelled humans to intervene and relocate the young bulls and females to Pilanesberg Park; the adult males were too large to be transported at the time. Soon after, numerous incidents of rhinos being attacked and killed began emerging from the area. Since the horns were still intact, officials knew it was not the work of poachers, and gradually it emerged that the unlikely suspects were the young bulls who had been moved there from Kruger.

Now, elephants don't usually gang up and kill other animals. These unusual events prompted an investigation which revealed that in the absence of the adult bulls, who traditionally have helped the adolescent bulls regulate behaviour, the young bulls were like teen gangs pumped up on testosterone! Their aggression went unchecked

---

[17]'The Delinquents,' *60 Minutes*, 22 August 2000, https://www.cbsnews.com/news/the-delinquents/, accessed 28 June 2021.

and unregulated because, practically, there was no one to teach them how to *be* elephants! These young bulls had entered maturity without any significant modelling about *how* to be an adult male elephant.[18] Thankfully, people were able to find a solution to the problem. They introduced a group of adult bulls into Pilanesberg Park and almost immediately saw the younger population become calmer and their behaviour more controlled. The killings stopped, and the young bulls were able to regulate their behaviour.

Gus van Dyk, the field ecologist at Pilanesberg Park, made a profound statement, 'I think everyone needs a role model, and these elephants that left the herd had no role model and no idea of what appropriate elephant behaviour was.'[19]

So, what does a herd of elephants teach us about people, role models and leadership in today's world?[20]

The absence of stable and robust role models can be as devastating in the human population as in the animal world. We may not all attack and kill, but much is lost when leaders develop without adequate role modelling of what that really means.

The flip side is that much is gained when we have role

---

[18]Ibid.

[19]Ibid.

[20]It's actually quite remarkable how similar the emotional worlds of elephants and humans can be.

To show that elephants experience the same emotions another is feeling, scientists watched captive Asian elephants in a park in Thailand. They noted when one elephant was upset by something, such as by a snake in the grass, and they recorded her behaviours to see if there was a pattern.

There was. In response to a stressful event, an elephant flares out her ears, erects her tail, and sometimes makes a low rumble. Scientists watching elephants in the wild have reported the same behaviours.

(Morell, Virginia, 'It's Time to Accept That Elephants, Like Us, Are Empathetic Beings,' *National Geographic*, 23 February 2014, https://www.nationalgeographic.com/animals/article/140221-elephants-poaching-empathy-grief-extinction-science, accessed on 3 August 2021.)

models to learn from: how to be human, how to be men and women, how to be professionals and how to be leaders of self and others.

While growing up, through college and the first years as professionals, we are bombarded by questions such as 'Who is your role model?' 'Who do you want to be like?' or 'Who inspires you?' At some point or the other, we have all asked others and ourselves these questions. In a socially bonded species like ours, learning from one another doesn't come as a surprise.

Seeking out the perspectives of those you trust is a great way to get an honest assessment of how people experience you. For this reason alone I would recommend everyone to have one or two role models or mentors in their life. Besides, when people share stories of their lives, we learn from their journeys, we are given a unique opportunity to learn without actually going through the challenges they experienced.

Neuro-linguistic Programming (NLP) confirms that we learn more by observing and imitating than in formal classrooms and workshops. We experience resonance when we meet someone who brings in shared experiences. Such experiences engage all of us. We are present in our thoughts, feelings and willingness to act—and that is the best learning there is. Changing behaviour or adopting new ones does not meet with much resistance then. This is also why we must choose our role models carefully and why leaders must be mindful of their behaviours in an organization.

Many of us know the importance of role models and would even go as far as to seek them out, but often, we do not know what we are looking for. That being the case, it is difficult to recognize people who would serve as good role models even if they may be right in front of us!

While choosing a suitable role model would depend a lot on what you are seeking to achieve, there are certain things that underpin the idea of a role model. It would help to seek out people who are:

- Good performers who display humility
- Accomplished yet approachable
- Interested in developing and motivating people
- Able to show genuine interest in your work
- Always seen raising the bar
- Willing to dedicate time and resources to you and follow through on commitments

We often think that a person in a leadership position will be the most likely role model, and while that is right at times, other people we have self-selected can be more influential than a formal leadership.

If you find yourself struggling to identify a role model, it might be a good idea to speak with your seniors and see if they can connect you with a suitable person. No one can do it all alone and seeking out support is essential to take charge of your professional growth and development.

Often, a conversation with a facilitator or fellow participants in a developmental workshop or learning setting can also set the ball rolling. Looking outside of your own business environment is also an accepted practice since you are looking to build perspective, character and identity through these conversations. You do not always need someone fluent in your domain. And sometimes, if all else fails and you must wait for a role model to show up in your life, it is a good practice to read the life stories of well-known leaders and draw inspiration from them.

Preparing to Be a Role Model

Just like you inadvertently look to your immediate senior to be the role model you seek, similarly, your team will look to you. This can seem intimidating to a person taking on this role for the first time, but developing ease and comfort with this space is

THE ELEPHANT
AT THE
DINNER TABLE

Praise for the Book

This book is an excellent piece of work. I enjoyed reading the personal experiences that have been shared so vividly. In addition, a great heart is displayed in the narration, making it very interesting and enriching. I recommend the book to students and management folks.

—**Clifford M. Pai**, V.P., H.R. Head. APAC & EMEA and
Global Head–Employee Relations, Infosys BPM

As Stephen King said, 'Books are a uniquely portable magic', and this is what Amit has achieved with this book. It will transport you to a world of real-life situations and narratives, as if you are there in person. I love how Amit has kept the writing simple yet so effective.

There is no bookish 'gyan' in this book. All the anecdotes and stories are real-life experiences, making them very relatable. Amit has deftly squeezed the entire experience and knowledge of his 31 years of work experience into this book for readers to learn from. Once you start reading, you can't stop. This book will be a quick reference guide for many of us in various professional and personal situations.

—**Nitin Arora**, Director, Government and Public Sevices, KPMG (India)

Amit's personality shines through in this book. I thoroughly enjoyed all the examples from his experience. As I read the book I could also visualize Amit delivering a compelling training session based on it.

—**Rochelle Kopp**, Japanese business culture expert and
cross-cultural communications specialist

The language is lucid, the content is easily relatable and the vocabulary is simple, making the book an easy read. In addition, the story concept is short and crisp and brings out the message very quickly.

—**Ankit Nagpal**, Manager, Learning & Leadership Development,
SKF India

I found the book highly practical and a companion that can enable you to improve relationships, communication and employee engagement. Amit offers a direct face-off between the manager and the leader by explaining that leaders must focus on their strengths to create engagement. I strongly recommend this book.

—**Rakesh Malhotra**, President and CEO, Global Natural Resources Inc.

It is truly a scholarly work involving research and analysis on the topic of leadership. I have no hesitation in recommending this as a primary text for students of management. The book offers faculty an excellent opportunity to engage students through discussions involving the real-life stories covered. It is also an excellent book to read for practising managers to gain new insights.

—**Prof. A.K.N. Prasad**, Former Head of Management
Development Centre, We school

This book leaves the reader with many intriguing questions to ponder about and with practical and easy-to-implement learnings. I felt like a co-traveller reading the anecdotes Amit has shared from his life experiences and the wisdom they offer. I would recommend the book to all working professionals looking at taking their leadership to the next level.

—**Nancy Katyal**, Executive Presence Coach,
Public Speaker, Leadership Facilitator

This creation is like an 'MBA (Leadership) in a box', with a lucid narration of stories, insightful nuggets of learning and unique introspective components. I am sure emerging leaders would be able to live back these stories as they go through their journey, just as existing leaders would have several very similar experiences to which they can relate.

—**Soumya Chakraborty**, Program Head–G&T
Leadership Development, Tata Consultancy Services

critical for your team as well as professional development.

One factor that sets a leader apart at this stage is domain knowledge. As you climb the corporate ladder, this might change, and your focus will become more strategic, but at this point in your career, having a solid grasp of your area of expertise is essential to gain your team's respect. They will not follow you or the examples you set if the reference is absent.

Also, taking the time to develop your communication capacity is essential. People sometimes, and erroneously, see this as an inessential add-on. All aspects of leadership can be traced back to good communication. The capacity to inspire and influence, create alignments and navigate tricky dynamics requires a leader to communicate well. As has been said earlier, communication is not limited to language skills; it includes the personal presence and impact that a leader makes. Do they only use words, or do they have a powerful *voice* with which they command our attention?

The keenness a leader displays to learning and acquiring new skills, gaining certifications, reading and developing his leadership persona also makes him a suitable role model.

Reverse Mentoring

Story #11

Seeking advice or inputs from people working for you has its own unique advantages. I recall, in 1998, when I was in two minds while deciding between opportunities to enhance my career by joining a pharmaceutical company or a new-age ITeS world, my discussion with a junior colleague helped me make the right choice. I vividly remember her giving me a nudge by reminding me of a training session wherein I encouraged the audience to be open to opportunities, narrating an analogy of a parachute that works only if it's open. My colleague, Bani Jolly, reminded me to practise what I was preaching in my training sessions. I vividly recall her saying, 'Sir, you have always taught us to have an open mind, with the parachute example.' I am so thankful for this discussion and the nudge that triggered my entry into the BPM world and a deeply fulfilling career.

GE's Jack Welch used Reverse Mentoring to teach senior executives about the Internet. Organizations such as BNY Mellon, PricewaterhouseCoopers, Estée Lauder and Bharti Airtel have been early adapters of reverse mentoring.

However, many leaders are fearful of revealing their lack of knowledge to junior employees. But, if the fears are addressed explicitly, open sharing can be enriching.

Being open to peers functioning as your sounding board is also an idea worth exploring. I have always believed in the unique strengths each one of us is blessed with. Discussing ideas and seeking counsel from a fellow worker can help explore new possibilities. Being open to the fact that you may not have answers to all issues and seeking advice from a co-worker is helpful.

Peer mentoring relaxes the traditionally rigid lines between mentor and mentee for a more even playing field. The accounting firm, Deloitte, runs the Emerging Leaders Development Program, to shape future Deloitte leaders. Each participant is assigned a partner, principal or director sponsor who commits at least two years to help their protégés drive their own careers by understanding how to navigate their organization. KPMG, Infosys BPM with their buddy initiative and Intel are leading organizations that actively promote peer learning.

During a crisis, people scramble to understand what they should do in the situation, and how it will affect them and their families. It is because of this uncertainty that mentoring matters. While a mentor may not have answers to the questions troubling us, they can provide some time and space to catch our breath and vent some of the pent-up anxiety the situation has triggered.

Keep these pointers in mind:

- It is vital to keep communicating. Schedule check-ins via a video call if an in-person meeting is difficult.
- Focus on empathy. Ensure to utilize your emotional quotient to the fullest.
- Offer unconditional support to employees who are facing a difficult time at home or work.

Argentinian player Lionel Messi, one of the most famous names in football and a master of his craft, had confessed in his interviews that French legend Zinedine Zidane was his role model. Messi said, 'And for role models, you have to look at Zidane. I loved to watch him, but he was such a hero in France, a great man away from football.' Now, don't you think Messi has outdone Zidane as a footballer?

Even the world's richest entrepreneur has role models. At a forum on leadership, Bezos said that he looked up to many people while growing up, such as his elementary school teachers, parents and grandfather. His grandfather was a 'gigantic influencer' in his life. In the business world, there are three CEOs the Amazon founder admires the most: Warren Buffett (billionaire investor and CEO of Berkshire Hathaway), Jamie Dimon (chairman of JP Morgan Chase) and Bob Iger (CEO of Disney).

Most organizations have review procedures to help their employees grow on the job. Those who want to become leaders can expect to be evaluated occasionally to see how they are doing, perhaps against set objectives. Many review procedures focus on employees' needs in development areas and their measures to correct inadequacies.

There is however a problem with this approach. Leaders are known for their strengths, not their weaknesses. As you grow towards leadership, take inventory of your strengths and find ways to nurture them. This is what makes you different, unique and valuable to your organization.

I like to work because that keeps me young.

This is what Prof A.K.N. Prasad mentioned to me over a discussion a few years ago. He served as the head of management development center at Welingkar Business School in Bengaluru. He has retired from this position last year.

I treat Prof A.K.N. as my mentor and also get inspired by the fact that several students continue to reach out to him for advice despite being in senior positions. Despite vision-related challenges, this gentleman continues to provide advice and direction to a leading business school and is also pursuing his passion for music.

Keep the momentum going. Keep taking actions.

If you believe in something, do it. And if it does not work out, it is always better to ask for forgiveness. I learnt this from T.K. Kurien, former CEO of Wipro Technologies, during our discussions on road travel.

For You to Reflect in Your Own Light

What key messages have stayed with you from the chapter?

_____

_____

_____

_____

Write down the names of all your role models. Who inspires you? What would you like to learn from them? (Older, younger or a peer). Build a cadre of people you can turn to for advice when you need it. Seek out the perspectives of those you trust to arrive at an honest assessment of how people experience you. I would recommend you have one or two role models or mentors in your life. Also, think of how you will nurture relationships with people whose perspectives you respect and value.

_____

_____

_____

_____

Look for a respectable person within the organization, someone who mirrors your career goals and helps you find the best fit. This may mean reaching out to someone in another office across the country or merely making an email introduction to a friend in the industry to help facilitate a coffee meeting. Engaging authentically on social media also helps.

_____

_____

_____

_____

Take a moment to reflect on what you are modelling for your team. Do you accept blame for your team but give credit where it is due, generally to others rather than yourself? Do you praise good performance in public but discuss poor performance in private? Think about your conduct from a third-person perspective.

_____

_____

_____

_____

_____

_____

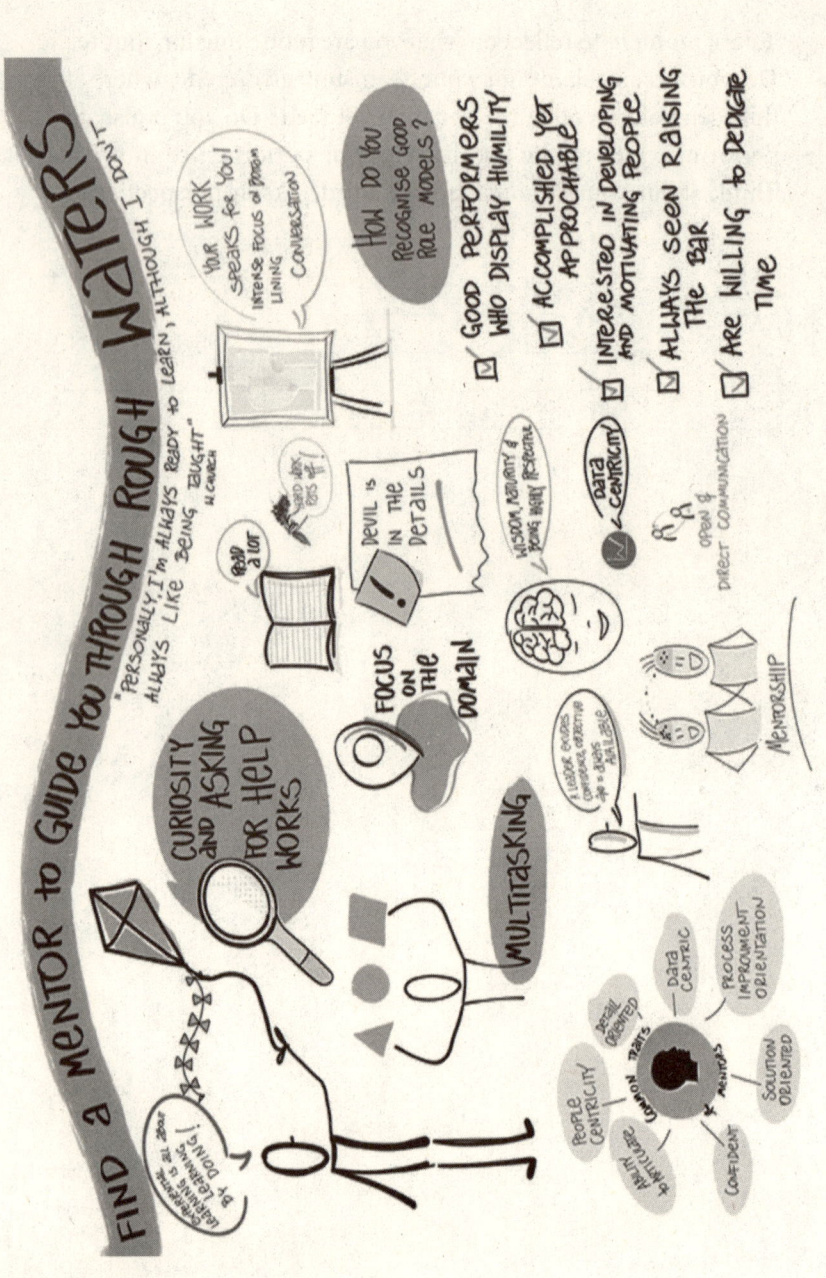

4

SHINE ON!

The key to human development is building on who you already are.

—Tom Rath, Author and consultant

As mentioned in the previous chapter, formal performance reviews scheduled periodically, along with the more informal comments of your supervisor every day, are designed to help you become a better leader by addressing your blind spots. Human resources (HR) departments are designed to develop talent and potential in their organization by providing more extensive training. Identifying potential and developing talent via performance reviews, training and related efforts keep HR departments running.

Identifying gaps in your training is something your supervisor can easily do. They know what training you have had in the past and can keep the HR department happy by suggesting additional training for you. It makes your supervisor's supervisor happy, too, because everyone is working to close performance development gaps.

But Is This the Right Decision?

It is funny that many organizations want to get better by modelling their employees' best practices—things that save time and/or money. But they fail to realize that the same holds true for the traits of their leaders. Every leader has a strength that made him or her a leader. It is a best practice among leaders in the company.

What I Learnt

We hear about leveraging potential and playing to our strengths almost every day in the corporate world, and yet, it astonishes me how often we are unaware of our natural strengths. I came remarkably close to missing a significant opportunity to align my work with my strengths. But, as luck would have it, the opportunity circled back 14 years later, and this time I was ready to grab it with both hands and a happy heart!

The Value of Persistence

Story #12

By 1996, I had spent seven years in the pharmaceutical industry, at GlaxoSmithKline, as a sales and marketing person. While, in some ways, I had found a place for myself and no longer suffered from the uncertainties that were the hallmark of my early working years, I was restless and eager to step into a leadership role. I had completed my sales and marketing diploma through Bharatiya Vidya Bhavan, New Delhi. Even though I could not complete my Master's in Business Administration (MBA)—not many leaders in the industry had an MBA at the time—I had hoped to finish the course and gain an edge. Till then, I planned to work closely and learn from the leaders around me. It paid off because they saw my enthusiasm and took the time to mentor me. Yet, despite my efforts, three separate attempts to get into an entry-level leadership role did not yield results, and I felt pretty upset.

Many people thought I would stay with Glaxo forever, and in a way, I did. After all, seven years is a long time. But the restlessness in me did not recede, and when I was called for an interview with Ranbaxy, one of India's leading pharmaceutical companies, I was quite thrilled.

Ranbaxy had set up a new business in a joint venture with the US pharmaceutical giant, Lilly, and was looking to take on more people. Rajeev Gulati, who was heading this unit, and was a perceptive and insightful man, conducted my interview. Within half an hour of the conversation, he stopped me mid-sentence and asked what I thought of training as a function. My skill at detailing the impact and benefits of various treatments appealed to him, and he felt I had the makings of a trainer in me.

Please remember that, at that time in the '90s, corporate functions such as training had not yet come into their own. In fact, at the time, it was widely accepted that people who could no longer serve as foot soldiers in sales would become trainers. Remember the old adage: 'Those who can't *do*, teach!' I was not thrilled by this question and addressed my interviewer directly. 'Mr Gulati, is this a polite way of saying I won't get this job?'

I did not get the sales job, but I did walk out of his office with the National Training Head's phone number, if I were interested in exploring the training field. I was not, and I did not make that call.

Within a few months of this interview, I finally earned a promotion at Glaxo and was sent to Ranchi, with Kolkata as my regional headquarter. This was when the political environment in the eastern part of our country was not very conducive to having a long-term career in the region. My promotion turned out to be a bit of a damper as I missed the action in the North. Hence, I began job hunting within a year of my being promoted. The opportunity of working as a sales trainer with one of our country's largest IT training companies was too tempting to let go of this time, especially with Gulati's words still echoing in my mind.

After Glaxo, the two years I spent at NIS Sparta as a sales trainer were amongst the finest in my career. I met two of my students in Hyderabad in 2018, while attending a national HR conference there. One of them works as a director in a global IT organization and the other gentleman is serving a legal processing organization at a senior level. No amount of money or fame can trigger such fulfilment as one experiences on seeing your students thrive in their careers.

Ever since my positive experiences at NIS, I always made it a point to soft negotiate some training-related work as a part of my more extensive job description in my future organizations. GECIS, where I worked as Associate Vice President (Operations) for over two years and Wipro BPM allowed me to hone my skills and take on additional talent-development roles. After GECIS, I joined Spectramind, which was acquired by Wipro in 2002. I worked at Spectramind for two years and at Wipro Spectramind for over three years, thus for over five years in all. At Wipro, I served as General Manager (Talent Development) for the western region for about a year, in 2005.

Gallup StrengthsFinder Assessment (now called CliftonStrengths)

So, you can imagine my surprise when, in 2010, the Gallup StrengthsFinder[21] revealed that I was most suited for a role in Training and Development! My love for learning, my lifelong pursuit of knowledge and the value I placed on it for my team, made me a natural candidate.

The five Gallup 'Signature Themes' that emerged for me were:

- Relator
- Communication
- Woo
- Positivity
- Individualization

These themes affirm that I am more suitable to play the role of a facilitator, consultant, coach and capability developer. I recently retook this assessment—after a decade—and it further reinforced my consulting and facilitation strengths.

The quote from Paulo Coelho's book, *The Alchemist*, that 'when you want something, all the universe conspires in helping

---

[21]In 2001, *Gallup* unveiled the *Gallup's* StrengthsFinder in a book titled *Now Discover Your Strengths* by Marcus Buckingham and Donald O. Clifton. This was the result of a landmark 30-year research project that ignited a global conversation on the topic of strengths. More than 10 million people have since taken *Gallup's* StrengthsFinder assessment. The revised StrengthsFinder was released in 2007 and has been named the Clifton StrengthsFinder in memory of Donald O. Clifton.

you to achieve it' came true for me. In 2010, I earned the role of Head of Training at Infosys BPM, through a series of actions:

- My follow-up with Swaminathan 'Swami' (former CEO and MD of Infosys BPM)
- Understanding the Gallup report
- Seeking inputs on the job from peers
- Intense interviews with Mr Vaitheeswaran 'Vaithee' (senior VP, Infosys), Raghavendra 'Raghu' (HR Head, Infosys), Srikatan 'Tan' Murthy (VP and Head of Learning, Infosys Technologies) and finally, Nandita Gurjar (HR Head, Infosys Technologies).

The result? Several prestigious awards and global appreciations followed and so did invitations to advisory committees and international events as a panelist and speaker, and of course, fulfilling work. Six fulfilling years in the same role—Head of Training at Infosys BPM, never a dull day!

For me, it validates Clifton's words, 'A leader needs to know his strengths as a carpenter knows his tools, or as a physician knows the instruments at her disposal. What great leaders have in common is that each truly knows their strengths and can call on the right strength at the right time. This explains why there is no definitive list of characteristics that describes all leaders.'[22]

Knowing your strengths is the hallmark of all leaders. The strengths may differ and they invariably do, but it is the *knowledge* that is the differentiator for a good leader. All leaders have a clear understanding of their potential and work towards harnessing them. Investing time and energy to discover strengths in self and others is a leader's primary task.

---

[22]Rath, Tom and Barry Conchie, 'Finding Your Leadership Strengths,' *Workplace*, 11 December 2008, https://www.gallup.com/workplace/237038/finding-leadership-strengths.aspx#:~:text=A%20leader%20needs%20to%20know,strength%20at%20the%20right%20time, accessed 10 July 2021.

As I reflect on Mr Gulati's advice and the Gallup Signature themes, I am reminded of my school days, when I would shut myself in a room and address an imaginary audience. What a correlation of data! It can't be just a coincidence, right?

We can sometimes get overly focused on what is not working and what needs repair. From a very early age, we are told what we need to improve or work on, such as our handwriting, our manners and our conduct, among other things. Our strengths or positives are simply glossed or skimmed over. Very naturally, that orients us to focus on the negatives, our so-called weaknesses. Even evolution has predisposed us to look at what is negative—'humans were designed to be keenly aware of negative circumstances and consequences as it helped their ancestors survive.'[23] So, survival demanded a strong sense of where the real danger or threat lay. While this was relevant millions of years ago, being unaware of your strengths is not an option in today's context. Know your strengths and be proud of them. At the same time, chase your dreams using your strengths as a fulcrum. As the professional certified coach Margaret Greenberg once said that carving out a role that speaks to your strengths will make you feel fulfilled and successful.

During my conversation with Sam Swaminathan, he commented that not all of us are aware of our strengths. He recommended that we seek out moments of reflection and ask ourselves one important question: what turns me on? Try to find out what excites you. Consciously try to do a self-discovery. This exercise can throw some light, especially in the absence of various assessment tools. Curiosity about self can help immensely. On top of it, if one can seek validation and recommendations via mentors, someone who can guide you, be a sounding board, it can be of great help.

---

[23]Jain, Renee, 'Why It's So Easy to Be Negative (and What to Do about It),' *HuffPost*, 6 December 2017, https://www.huffpost.com/entry/negativity-bias_b_3517365, accessed 29 June 2021.

A True Leader Invokes Positive Actions

Story #13

Sam reinforced his message through real-life experiences. In the early '70s, he served the Navy. During one of his trips, the ship he was sailing had a major technical glitch. It had to be docked for repairs in Mumbai for a long duration. Until the ship got repaired, he found a very stable 9 to 5 role for himself, with nothing much to do after five in the evening except play billiards and snooker. Commander Roy, who lived in the same residential complex, would watch Sam taking long evening strolls along with his wife daily.

He became curious and, at the same time, disappointed in Sam idling away his time. He encouraged Sam to utilize his time better and enrol in a management programme. The senior officer helped him get transferred to the Mumbai unit so that Sam could continue his studies and complete his management programme from the prestigious Jamnalal Bajaj Institute of Management Studies. The encouragement from his wife and support from the officer were a turning point in Sam's life. He discovered his core strengths and pursued a career in management and consulting. He always feels indebted to Commander Roy for having faith in him and for helping him step out of the comfort zone.

Diving Deep: Research Insights

What Do We Mean by 'Strengths'?

We can sometimes confuse strengths with what we are naturally good at or things we like doing. While there is a bit of that too, I like how Gallup explains it: 'Strength is not the same as a talent, but it is identifying dominant talents and then complementing them by acquiring skills and knowledge that buttress the capacity to show results in that area repeatedly and consistently.'[24]

A sportsperson might have a natural inclination or *talent* for a sport. Yet, it is the time and energy spent in acquiring the expertise and skill set to consistently and repeatedly replicate good performance that actually constitutes one's strength. There is an active element of *action* that allows a talent or interest to become a strength, a true potential.

Martin Seligman, the father of positive psychology, defines strengths as traits that can be acquired, while talents are innate. According to him, moral strengths such as integrity, honesty and will also value *action* and will be seen over time, across a situation, and in the tangible behaviours.[25]

Talents can only take you so far. Talent is like the raw material we are born with. If someone is born with an ear for music and another is tone-deaf, the first individual is more suited to a career in music. Strengths, however, are what we build along the way. When we are aware of our talents and aptitudes and then learn skills to hone them, they become our strengths. In my case, though it took quite some time to earn a full-time role in Training and Development, I ensured to persevere and negotiate additional responsibilities around process capabilities/training in the various roles I assumed at GE, Wipro and Infosys.

---

[24]I had picked this up from my notes captured during a *Gallup* training programme several years back.

[25]Seligman, Martin E.P., *Authentic Happiness: Using the New Positive Psychology to Realize Your Potential for Lasting Fulfillment* (Atria Books; Reprint edition, 2004).

Strengths are like muscles. If we stop developing our strengths, they can atrophy and become weak. Even an abstract strength, like personal integrity, can weaken over time if we do things that go against our sense of integrity.

There is a fantastic article on Gallup.com that talks about how *strength is* actually a *language* used to deepen the connection and mutual understanding between dispersed global teams.[26] As I have shared earlier, the Gallup approach to strengths makes sense to me, and I approve of the reason why it promotes strengths as the international language.[27] It seems counter-intuitive and perfectly obvious at the same time!

1. When people talk about their strengths, it is easier to create a safe space for people to open up. Once they have bonded over strengths, there is a greater willingness to reveal vulnerabilities and areas of struggle.

2. The language of strengths creates a positive impact—a sense of *flow*—because working with strength areas is more manageable and does not need as much effort as when we struggle to overcome a 'weakness'.

3. Using a standard assessment tool across the organization allows employees across the globe to have a common language to share their best attributes with each other. Talking about how they think or behave similarly or differently from each other can be a great way to break through natural resistances between people from vastly different contexts.

4. People are naturally drawn to discover who they are,

---

[26]'Strengths: A Global Language,' *Gallup*, 10 May 2007, https://news.gallup.com/businessjournal/27457/strengths-global-language.aspx, accessed 10 July 2021.

[27]'Why Create a Strengths-Based Company Culture?' *Gallup*, https://www.gallup.com/cliftonstrengths/en/290903/how-to-create-strengths-based-company-culture.aspx, accessed 29 June 2021.

how they can bring value to their work and how best to leverage their talents—thus providing a platform where these conversations can create positive energy around teams and individuals.

5. When looking to transition from one role to another, knowing which strengths allow you to perform well in your role helps you assess how you can leverage them in future. This also enables you to identify the skills you will have to acquire to perform better. When we know our key strengths, we can transition relatively quickly and effortlessly.

6. Employers often attribute attrition to the income increments that companies offer. However, an article by Gallup identifies that people usually change to jobs that allow them to do what they do best, i.e., work to their strengths, than to jobs that offer higher pay.[28]

7. We have talked about creating engagement for our teams and ourselves; a Gallup survey shows a direct link between engagement and our capacity to identify and use our strengths at work.[29]

Know your strengths, own your strengths.

—Marcus Buckingham, Author and motivational speaker

In my experience, very few people take the time to know their

---

[28]Mann, Annemarie and Amy Adkins, 'The Dream Job,' *Gallup*, 1 March 2017, https://news.gallup.com/businessjournal/204533/dream-job.aspx, accessed 10 July 2021.

[29]Brim, Brian J., 'How a Focus on People's Strengths Increases Their Work Engagement,' *Gallup*, 2 May 2019, https://www.gallup.com/workplace/242096/focus-people-strengths-increases-work-engagement.aspx#:~:text=Many%20research%20studies%20allude%20to,to%207%25%20higher%20customer%20engagement, accessed 10 July 2021.

strengths, and those who do are almost always successful—not just in their career but in their personal life too. Over time, we get better at adapting to changes and transition, and it is essential to periodically check in with ourselves and see where we stand.

Since most successful leaders put effort into developing and using their strengths while simultaneously managing their weaknesses, being able to identify your strengths and encouraging people in your team to do the same is unbelievably valuable. It is essential to keep in mind that our strengths are often intangible or abstract and can be easily missed if we do not know what we are looking for. Optimism, hope and the resilience to overcome setbacks and frustrations can sometimes get missed if we only see our abilities and skills to *do* tangible things as strengths.

Self-assessments such as the 'Brief Strengths Test' created by Martin Seligman at www.authentichappiness.org[30] or Gallup's StrengthsFinder assessment[31] take just a few minutes to complete and measure various strengths. You can also buy relevant books and understand how you can positively use this information. Once you have your list of strengths ready, one way to go about it is to ask yourself the following questions:

- In what areas of my life do I use these strengths?
- How can I use more of my strengths, so I am more fulfilled in what I do?
- What has made me stay in a role where I have not used my strengths?
- What was the result or outcome of that role?

Asking other people for direct and honest feedback is also an excellent way to get inputs on your strengths. Choose five people

---

[30]'Take a test here: Authentic Happiness, University of Pennsylvania,' https://www.authentichappiness.sas.upenn.edu/testcenter, accessed 29 June 2021.
[31]'Live Your Best Life Using Your Strengths,' *Gallup*, https://www.gallup.com/cliftonstrengths/en/home.aspx, accessed 29 June 2021.

who know you well and are not afraid to talk straight. Make sure they have an insight into your professional world and then look for commonalities across responses. Be open to what they have to say and you could end up with a robust list of what you do well.

Weaknesses as Areas of Stretch

Despite what you have read so far, ask yourself, 'How much time do I spend reflecting on things that I'm not good at?' Be honest to yourself. You will be surprised at the answer. Given this inclination and the cultural leaning towards highlighting 'areas of improvement', it is essential to state that a strengths focus does not mean we turn a blind eye to what we struggle with or are not particularly good at. Ignorance of limitations is a great way to have them blow up in your face! By knowing your blind spots, you can engage in timely and appropriate course correction.

For me, the dream of completing an MBA has not yet been realized. Initially, I could not afford it, and then I was accepted into two universities but could not attend due to circumstances. When I finally did enroll, relocation and demands of the job made it impossible to complete the programme. However, one of my greatest strengths is being able to connect with people and sustain relationships. I am still connected with fellow students (now great friends) from the Symbiosis Institute of Business Management, where I was briefly enrolled in the Executive MBA programme in 2004.

It is one of the top-rated business schools in India. My hands-on learning began with talking to people, associating with those more knowledgeable, reading and experimenting—everything I am naturally inclined towards and good at. My desire for learning was channelled through these avenues, and it built enough momentum for me to reach where I am today. For a couple of years, I went back to this business school, contributing via guest lectures and assessment centres.

I find that focusing too much on our 'weaknesses' can paralyse us into inaction. And, as Jack Welch has often said, 'I find that the cost of inaction is usually higher than taking action, realizing it is not yielding the desired results and quickly course correct. It is essential to know that at work, as in life, things will go wrong more often than they go right, but that cannot come in the way of *doing*. Focusing on "fixing" weaknesses often does precisely that—it prevents us from making decisions and taking action because all our energy is focused on "getting it *right*" or at the very least "*not* getting it *wrong*"!'[32]

Having said that, sometimes I still want those three letters, MBA, attached to my name and given the right time and circumstances, I might pursue that dream. The energy I bring to my dream and work today is quite different, I am curious and eager. Had I allowed the absence of the degree to define me and hold me back, I doubt if I would have made the choices and seen the successes that I have today.

In 2017, I learnt a new word to address our weaknesses, referred to as 'stretch areas'. I find this word very positive and action-oriented. Jonathan Halls, my trainer at the ATD Master Trainer Program, used this term while sharing feedback on our demos during the sessions.

To further explore this topic, I highly recommend the book *Strengths Based Leadership*[33]. Thirty years of intensive research by Gallup scientists, as interpreted by best-selling author Tom Rath and outstanding leadership and performance coach Barry Conchie, culminated in this book. The book's authors had access

---

[32]I learnt about the action-centric approach through my interactions with Raman Roy. Raman had met Jack a few times and was close to some of the leaders reporting to Jack. Also heard about this need for action and his hate towards procrastination from my conversations with Mr T.K. Kurien.

[33]Rath, Tom and Barry Conchie, *Strengths Based Leadership: Great Leaders, Teams, and Why People Follow* (*Gallup* Press: 2008).

to over 40,000 personal interviews with leaders, 20,000 interviews with followers and surveys from nearly a million work teams worldwide. They discovered that teams were most successful when the 'Four Leadership Domains' of relationship building, strategic thinking, influencing and executing were covered.[34]

The leadership evaluation identifies your top five leadership strengths and guides you on applying these strengths to meet your followers' four basic needs—trust, compassion, stability and hope.

Remember the Gallup's Signature Themes identified for me by Gallup consultants while at Infosys? I personally found this quite helpful and highly encourage all leaders to take one for themselves. Even if you are aware of your strengths, this assessment further validates your knowledge of the same and provides you with tips to further develop your potential.

Facebook is a great example where strengths-based leadership is applied at several levels. Their non-traditional approach in

[34]To help identify strengths as a leader, the book comes with a leadership evaluation code at https://www.gallup.com/cliftonstrengths/en/strengthsfinder.aspx.

candidate recruitment is quite interesting. Sometimes, it finds the best talent in the industry and brings people on board without any particular role in mind. This approach allows them to match their skill set with their projects of interest.

Job rotation is another excellent practice adopted by the organization. Every 18 months or so, its engineers must rotate and work on something different for a while. This practice frequently brings new perspectives and experiences to the table and ignites new ideas. This practice also prevents the team from getting complacent in their respective roles. However, in doing so, it is essential not to force 'unnatural talent' or 'project pairing'.

The company encourages its workers to form teams around projects they are passionate about and have the most potent skill set linked to their strengths. The leadership understands and appreciates that great work comes from doing what you love and applying your strengths in innovative ways.

Anyone can be a hero due to the flat organization structure, wherein irrespective of your job title or role, if you have the best idea, you are celebrated.

Facebook also holds hackathons, monthly all-nighters, where any idea or project can be brought forth for others to improve the platform. New features, updates to usable codes and many other process improvements are discovered and shared through such initiatives. Employees treat this as an intellectual and creative exercise. The only rule is that during hackathons, one can work only on someone else's project. Some of the most popular site features, such as chat, video messaging and timeline came out of these hackathons.

3M is another company that allows its employees to apply their strengths in the projects and ideas they are passionate about. We have all heard about companies such as Google allowing employees the time and encouragement to create. Still, it is a little-known fact that 3M set a precedent for this practice years before with its '15 percent time'—a programme that allows people who work at 3M to use a portion of their weekly work time to create and develop their own ideas. As a matter of fact, the programme has produced many of 3M's best-selling products, including the Post-it-note. In 1974, Art Fry, a scientist at 3M, came up with that famous but straightforward invention.

Strength-based leadership is often overlooked. Primarily because of the 'we-have-always-done-it-this-way' syndrome. Once we understand the value of improvement and fierce competition, we can become better versions of ourselves. However, breeding more leaders, not more just mediocre managers, would need revisiting how people are hired, and how teams are built and managed.

Strength-based leadership is about lifting your people's vision to new horizons, their performance to higher standards and building of their personality beyond its normal limits.

—Clifford M. Pai, VP, H.R. Head.
APAC & EMEA and Global Head–Employee
Relations, Infosys BPM

◆

Executive Presence has the extraordinary power to unlock the hero in each one of us. It is only through unleashing your presence that you can realize your full leadership potential.

—Nancy Katyal, Executive Presence Coach,
Public Speaker, Leadership Facilitator

For You to Reflect in Your Own Light

What key messages have stayed with you from the chapter?

_____

_____

_____

_____

_____

_____

Here's a series of exercises you can do to discover your best self:

Step 1: Identify people whose opinion you value and ask for feedback.

The exercise's first task is to collect feedback about yourself at your best from various people inside and outside of work. If you want to recognize your strengths, you need to hold up a mirror. Who can be the mirror-holders for you?

By gathering input from various sources—family members, past and present colleagues, friends, teachers and so on—you can develop a much broader and richer understanding of yourself than you can from a standard performance evaluation. Reflect in writing the responses you receive. (Tip: try soliciting feedback on emails; it's easy to cut and paste answers into an analysis table)

_____

_____

_____

_____

_____

_____

Step 2: Recognize patterns.

In this step, search for common themes among the feedback you have received and add examples with your own observations. Now organize all the input into a table. Creating a table will help you make sense of the feedback. By clustering examples, you can compare responses and identify common themes more easily.

Here is a sample table for your understanding:

Common theme	Examples given	Possible interpretation

(This step can be genuinely illuminating; it sheds light on things we know about ourselves and also aspects that we take for granted.)

Step 3: Compose your self-portrait.

Write a description of yourself that summarizes what the analysis revealed, weaving the themes from the feedback and your own observations into a composite of your 'personal best'. It should be a prose composition approximately three paragraphs long. Please begin the first paragraph with the statement, 'When I am at my best, I...' This will take time and careful consideration but should provide an image of who you are now and what you are capable of becoming.

(Remember, this is not a psychological profile but will provide an insightful image that you can use to recall your previous contributions and guide future action.)

_____
_____
_____
_____
_____
_____
_____

Step 4: Reflect on your career path and redesign your job.

Having pinpointed your strengths, your next step should be to redesign your personal job description. It will be useful to write down a personal job description that is linked with your strengths.

_____
_____
_____
_____
_____
_____

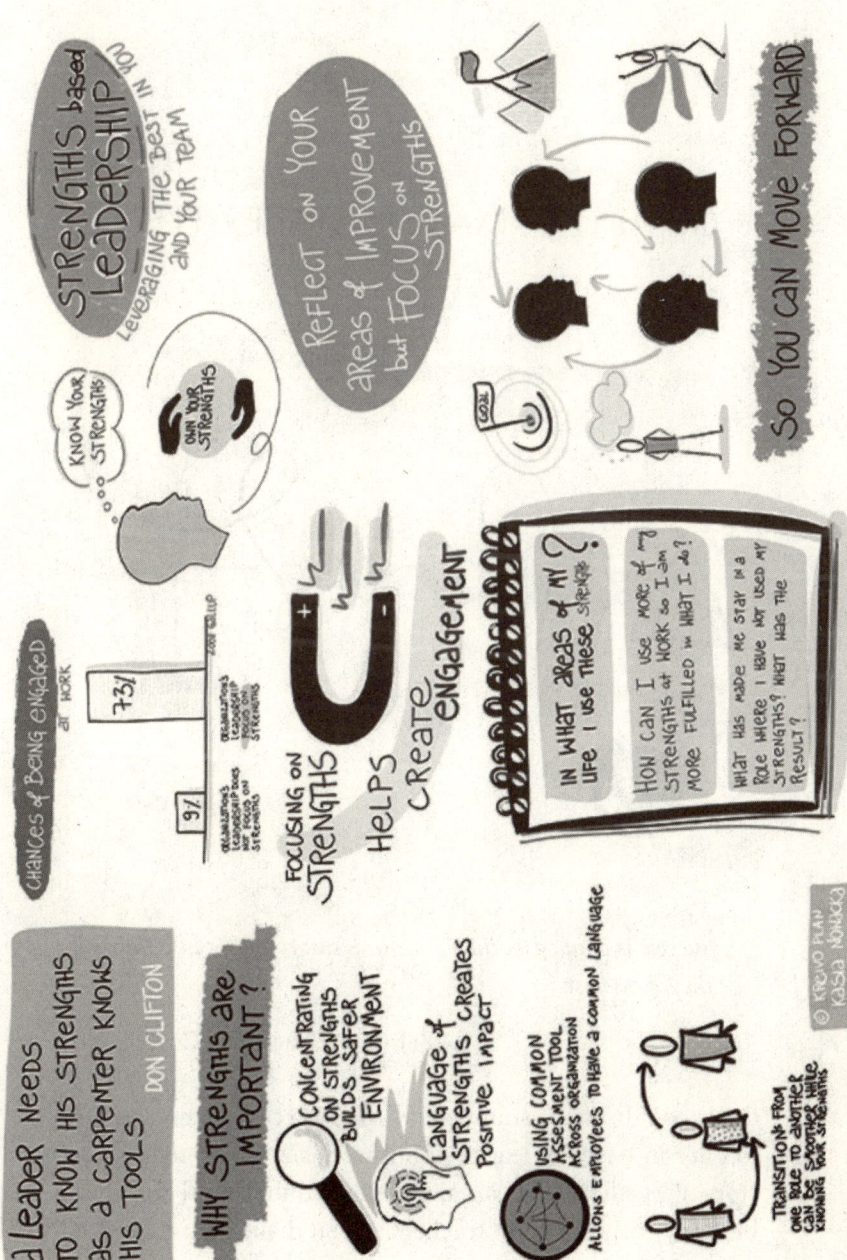

5

GO AHEAD, MAKE MISTAKES, PLEASE!

Success is a lousy teacher. It seduces smart people into thinking they can't lose.

—Bill Gates, Microsoft Co-Founder

Gates couldn't have summed it better. Success doesn't have much to offer in terms of learning. But mistakes—now, that is another story altogether. Mistakes are often misunderstood and shunned, but they truly are great teachers. If you make a mistake, you can look at it two ways: get depressed and fear the future, or learn from it.

Believe it or not, some organizations actually encourage people to make mistakes. They see the value and progress that occurs as a result. Today, mistakes have earned a new level of respect.

What I Learnt

'You have goofed-up', 'you have got it wrong' or 'you have dropped the ball' are phrases that can strike fear in the best of us. And as leaders, we dread hearing them. We take failures and mistakes very personally. And even though we try to convince ourselves that it's OK and everyone makes a mistake every now and again, deep in our hearts, we don't let ourselves off the hook and instead resolve to be more cautious, more guarded and consequently, less leader-like.

Taking risks and making decisions, often with limited information and scarce resources, is the leader's daily work. And the fact of the matter is, sometimes we *will* get it wrong. I never fail to wonder what would happen if, instead of spending all our energy on *trying* not to make a mistake, we spent that energy on becoming good at recognizing, acknowledging and rectifying our errors where possible. What would happen if we were kinder to ourselves and more proactive in our actions rather than beating ourselves up and freezing or fleeing?

Mistakes can be costly; there is no doubt about that. But being a leader who shies away from risks because of the fear of errors or cannot own up to their mistakes, is costlier. This applies to both the individual and the organization.

I remember one of the mistakes I made in the early days of my career. Picture this: It is 1989, and India is just about to open its economic borders to the world. After Pandit Nehru took office as our first prime minister we have had manufacturing industries and employee unions, but we had not yet got the hang of how corporate spaces work. I had just joined Glaxo and was looking to find my niche, my identity. I was looking to belong in this new space to spend most of my waking hours in. So, I talked to as many people and attended as many engagements and events as I could. I was hungry to know the world around me and get involved.

Gaining from Rookie Errors

Story #14

A few months into work, I found myself attending one of the events organized by the Federation of Medical and Sales Representatives' Associations of India, a Communist Party of India (Marxist)-socialist party wing of sorts. Innumerable cups of tea and several conversations with the Federation members at the company canteen culminated in my being invited to the event and I was excited to attend it. Now, remember, I was young, new to the organization and looking to fit in. The invitation sounded terrific and I readily accepted it. What I had not counted on was to find myself at a *dharna* (protest meeting) in a face-off with the regional manager at Glaxo! Since I had joined the trade union, I found myself at a protest meeting outside our regional office, thus embarrassing my regional manager, who had high hopes for me.

It took me close to a year to mend fences after that encounter. I distanced myself from this representative's association and started focusing a lot more on my work. Through my renewed focus, hard work and regular communication with my leaders, I was able to restore their confidence in my abilities. And here, I want to specify that, while it's perfectly fine to join a union or any group *per se,* it's crucial to check whether these choices align with the larger professional goals you may have set for yourself. My mistake was the lack of clarity with which I jumped into things.

I wanted to get into management at Glaxo and yet was lured by the idea of belonging to a group, *any* group for that matter. I did not take into consideration whether this group aligned with the goals I set for myself.

I had no desire to antagonize the management, but I took what I thought was a social opportunity and made a political faux pas. It was a rookie mistake, and it taught me to be clear with my values and then choose to align with a group, idea or action plan.

There were other mistakes, thankfully on a smaller scale. Many were made at Glaxo. I suppose that was because the organization was one of my first learning grounds. I remember going for my interview in 1988 and not carrying my resume! I asked for a sheet of paper and wrote out my skill sets, only to realize that my handwriting ran diagonally across the paper, instead of in straight lines! I will never forget the look of displeased annoyance on the face of the interview coordinator. Nevertheless, I got the job, clearing multiple rounds of interviews and learnt an invaluable lesson on the virtues of preparedness.

Mistakes Come in Different Sizes

The scale of mistakes in organizations can vary, often depending on your position and authority to make decisions. While young leaders will not be asked to make strategic decisions around product launches or to acquire another company, they will be accountable for the range of decisions they are expected to make in their respective roles. Mistakes that new leaders make stem from several reasons, such as a need to be liked, impulsive decision-making or short-sightedness instead of long-term thinking.[35] This can result in difficulties in giving direct feedback,

---

[35]'How to Quickly Overcome Inexperience,' *Leadership Freak*, 22 March 2012, https://leadershipfreak.blog/2012/03/22/how-to-quickly-overcome-inexperience/, accessed 29 June 2021.

addressing symptoms rather than seeking causes or forgetting to communicate the organizational vision.

While these reasons will continue to exist, mistakes will continue to be made. Anyone aspiring to be a leader will have to traverse this tricky path in their journey. 'Unless anyone is dead, this situation can be recovered. Therefore, visibly learn your lesson and move on. No one wants to follow leaders who can't admit having made a mistake,' says Bobby Chatterjee, Senior Director, HR, Hertz. Having certain signposts, a *perspective* to this journey, may help. Our view and understanding of a situation can help us navigate it with greater ease and self-assurance; else, we are likely to panic or even despair every time we hit a normal developmental milestone for a leader.

There are a few more mistakes that I would like to share. These mistakes helped me become humbler and increased my self-awareness and learning in my journey of becoming a better leader. Twice in my career, I experienced two stints with the same organization. Once at Wipro, and a second time, at Infosys. While both decisions of leaving these organizations were aimed at carving a better future for myself, it did not take me much time in realizing that I was short-changed for a better role and location. While I am incredibly grateful to be welcomed back and allowed to play more diverse and meatier roles, the lessons learnt on blind faith and limited due diligence before making a job shift, continue to serve me well even today.

During my interviews with Raman, he recollected the initial days of the set-up of Spectramind in 2000. His chief technology officer (CTO), Sunil Gujral, was a visionary and had set up internet-based voice IP (Internet Protocol) phones for the contact centre. Though this was a technology of the future, there were voice latency issues that impacted customer experience. The CTO had to revert to the traditional infrastructure to meet the client requirements. Raman could have taken a tough call with the CTO;

he, however, took the intent of setting up a futuristic network as innovative and sincere.

Celebrating Failure

Google rewards its employees, not just for their successes but also for their failures. According to a FastCompany.com article, Google employees are publicly applauded by their co-workers and supervisors for their failures.[36] They are often rewarded with time off to contemplate what their next project will be. But Google is not the only company that hails failure.

Supercell, the gaming company behind the popular online game, Clash of Titans, celebrates employee failures by cracking open champagne bottles! Can you believe it? And P&G, the billion-dollar global consumer goods giant, is known for its prestigious 'Heroic Failure Award', given to employees who took the greatest intelligent risk at the company.[37] Several other companies reportedly also have their own versions of the award. Tata group of companies has institutionalized 'Dare to Try' Innovista Awards to promote innovation.[38] Spotify, the music streaming company, has a 'Fail Wall' across its offices showcasing failure.[39]

But why on earth would companies credited for their

---

[36]'How Google's Moonshot X Division Helps Its Employees Embrace Failure,' Fast Company, 14 April 2016, https://www.fastcompany.com/3058866/how-googles-moonshot-x-division-helps-its-employees-embrace-failure, accessed 10 July.

[37]Johnson, Ron, 'Why Google rewards its employees for failing,' Linkedin, https://www.linkedin.com/pulse/why-google-rewards-its-employees-failing-ron-johnson/, accessed 29 June 2021.

[38]'Press Release: Tata companies showcase over 3,300 implemented innovations, doubling over two years,' 3 July 2017, https://www.tata.com/newsroom/tata-companies-showcase-3300-innovations-doubling-over-two-years, accessed 29 June 2021.

[39]Eriksson, Ulf, 'How Spotify Does Agile—A Look at The Spotify Engineering Culture,' http://reqtest.com/agile-blog/how-spotify-does-agile-a-look-at-the-spotify-engineering-culture/, accessed 29 June 2021.

successful track records and high rates of innovation, reward people for failing? Doesn't that encourage employees to lower their own expectations and, instead, produce mediocre work? Not so, say leaders from Google and many successful companies who encourage their team members to fail. These companies recognize that atychiphobia (the scientific name for 'irrational and persistent fear of failure') can be paralysing and a tremendous threat to their competitiveness.

Astro Teller, Director of X (formerly 'Google X'), believes that celebrating failure helps increase employee innovation. X is the research division of Google's parent company, Alphabet. In an interview with BBC, Teller said: 'If I make you feel stupid because you tried something new and it did not work out, you're never going to try something new again. But if we can create a culture together where you feel stupid because you have not tried something new this week, you're going to try something new every week.'[40]

Coffee That Left a Bitter Taste

Story #15

During my interview with Sam Swaminathan, he recalled an interesting anecdote. During a client meeting with a senior leader at UPS, his executive assistant brought coffee in a mug with FedEx, the competitor's logo prominently displayed! Sam was unhappy with his executive assistant and internally questioned his abilities. However, he was proven wrong when this faux pas was addressed in the subsequent meeting, wherein the same executive assistant served coffee using mugs with the freshly printed logo of their client, UPS. This act was received quite well by the client.

---

[40]Astro Teller on BBC TV, http://www.astroteller.net/press/appearances/astro-teller-on-bbc-tv, accessed 10 July 2021.

During the first meeting, Sam's executive assistant had sought their client's business card before he left and subsequently got the client company's logo scanned and organized for new mugs. According to Sam, he had clearly underestimated his resource, which was a mistake on his part.

In 2005–06, while transitioning from Wipro to Infosys, I took a leap of faith and set up my first consulting venture. With several promises made by ex-colleagues, acquaintances and a few friends, I made some incorrect assumptions, and as a result, the venture did not take off.

The key learnings from this experience were:

- High dependencies on my network
- An incorrect assumption of network worth
- Lack of clarity around offerings or products
- Cash flows of less than 24 months

It took me 10 years of preparation which included solid financial planning, to muster enough courage to take another plunge in 2016. During the first 18 months of the launch of my firm, Pursuitica, I failed to anticipate immense challenges concerning marketing a product versus training services. Additionally, global competition, and the associated marketing expenses, harmed my financial statements.

We sometimes have difficulty distinguishing trustworthy people from untrustworthy ones. I recall how we celebrated our partnership with a more prominent firm over dinner to be surprised the following day. The more prominent firm had made another offer to my technology partners the same night after the dinner and struck a deal with them. Meanwhile, this organization had already initiated an informal knowledge transfer from me. Hence, they had enough information to jumpstart.

However, taking a cue from the past learnings, I believe I am better prepared now. I persevered, upgraded my skills, made quick changes and invested in the future through better collaborations, deeper networks and associating with trustworthy organizations.

This time, I am glad to report a reasonably positive experience and quite an upbeat future!

Diving Deep: Research Insights

Is there comfort in never having made a mistake? Or is there that feeling that a big mistake is right around the corner? Should you not be aggressive for fear of committing that mistake? Is it possible to become comfortable with the notion of making the inevitable mistake?

Understanding Mistakes: Failure or Feedback?

As leaders and even as professionals, you might have been told to give yourself permission to make mistakes. This, however, might be harder than you imagine, significantly if you grew up or studied in an environment where there was a low tolerance for errors and if you have experienced harsh punishments each time you slipped up.

There is a balance, of course—becoming comfortable with making mistakes does not imply you get comfortable with repeatedly making the same mistakes or become unmindful or impulsive when making decisions. Usually, we place such a high premium on getting it right that we either freeze and procrastinate with decision-making or make reckless decisions and hope they go well. Success in both situations is left too much to chance.

There is a core principle in NLP which states that there is no failure, only feedback.[41] The idea of success and failure is value-laden and varies from context to context. If you view failure as just a response from the environment that tells you that this method is not working, then you expend more energy finding a plan that does. It took Thomas Edison a thousand tries to invent the light bulb, and he is famous for saying, 'I have not failed, not once. I've discovered one thousand ways that don't work.'

When we get stuck with the idea of having *failed*, we might feel small, inadequate, incompetent; we might deny, despair or find someone to blame. None of that is problem-solving. Understanding this principle can help constructively frame our approach to mistakes and focus our energy on course correction.

Path of Least Resistance: OK for Rivers

We all know that a leader's mistakes, especially at a strategic level, can prove enormously expensive for the individual, the team and the organization. The cost can be computed in terms of money, loss of esteem and loss of talented people. This cost can also be seen as a loss of credibility that has been built over the years.

People sometimes misunderstand this and do their best to *never make mistakes*, which usually translates to not taking enough risks. The play-it-safe mindset is antithetical to good leadership because how can one be creative, innovative or path-breaking if one never strays from the well-trodden trails? The wandering

---

[41]'There Is No Such Thing As Failure, Only Feedback,' http://nlpls.com/articles/failureVSfeedback.php, accessed 29 June 2021.

away from the familiar must be well thought through, and the risk must be a calculated one, but it is a risk, nonetheless. In this context, I would like to recall a comment by Gilles Hilary, an INSEAD Professor of Accounting and Control. He said, 'By continually putting yourself in a situation where you minimize risk when bad things happen—and bad things do happen from bad luck if nothing else—your ability to learn and recover is reduced.'[42] The path of least resistance is excellent for rivers, not so much for leaders.

It becomes critical that we define what is required to convert a *pure* mistake into a growth and learning opportunity. It is not the fact that you made a mistake that impacts your credibility; it is not taking ownership of it and rectifying it that hurts trust and credibility. When we take ownership of our behaviour, it shows integrity and builds credibility. The willingness to do it even at personal or organizational cost builds trust. [43]

I would like to invoke a quote from Warren Bennis, widely regarded as a pioneer of the contemporary field of leadership studies: 'Becoming a leader is synonymous with becoming yourself. It is precisely that simple, and it is also that difficult.' It's almost like a mantra.

When leaders understand the true meaning of his words, their approach to themselves, their team and their life changes. In life, as in leadership, learning to take responsibility for our mistakes is a process that takes time and self-reflection, and when done often enough and sincerely enough, it builds character, trust and credibility.

---

[42]Williams, Jane, 'Make Mistakes Part of Your Career Success,' INSEAD, 3 February 2015, https://knowledge.insead.edu/leadership-organisations/make-mistakes-part-of-your-career-success-3823#HwtjEHKRk8LZTkC.99, accessed 29 June 2021.

[43]Covey, Steven M., *The SPEED of Trust: The One Thing That Changes Everything* (Free Press: 2008).

Embracing Mistakes: Failing Forward

Contrary to popular belief, failure is not the opposite of success, rather it is a necessary part. In *Failing Forward*, John Maxwell writes that failure does not need to be avoided. Instead, it should be embraced because we can learn from it and become stronger in the future as a result.[44]

There are many reasons why it's challenging to own up to our mistakes. Sometimes, we don't even realize that the responsibility for something that went wrong lies with us. That's when blind spots get the better of us, and we would benefit from soliciting regular and honest feedback.

We may not see our mistakes because when presented with data, which goes against what we believe about the world or ourselves, it causes deep discomfort. This discomfort is known as cognitive dissonance. This clash of belief with reality needs to be resolved at the earliest moment to be comfortable again. If you hear yourself say, 'I couldn't have done that', 'That's not like me', or 'It can't have been', then you know you have come face-to-face with cognitive dissonance. We usually resolve this by dismissing the new data and justifying and reaffirming what we initially believed, even in evidence that it is incorrect. The more helpful approach would be to reassess the belief you hold so dearly and see if it still stands true or needs modification.

This pattern of human behaviour fits in well with another tendency, which is known as a confirmation bias, where we tend to only register and take cognisance of data that confirms our understanding of people and events of the world around us. This was an evolutionary requirement—when you went hunting for food, you didn't want to get distracted by the trees, the birds or flowers, so the mind learnt to focus and only take in data that

---

[44]Maxwell, John C., *Failing Forward: Turning Mistakes into Stepping Stones for Success* (HarperCollins Leadership: 2007).

allowed you to track and hunt, say a deer.

We find it hard to admit mistakes because, if we do, we will have to backtrack and start again. This is known as the sunk cost fallacy, where we believe that '*I have already invested so much (time, effort and resources) into this, I can't give up now*'. So, I might stay in a relationship or a job that no longer works for me simply because '*I've been here so long*'.

While researching this chapter, Mrinalini stumbled upon an interesting article on a website called '*The Art of Manliness*'[45] that explained quite simply why we struggle to own our mistakes. Now, while she would have loved a different name for the site, their intent and approach are worth mentioning. This article provides great insights and recommendations on this topic.

The cycles of denial and blame can undermine the hard-won credibility of an individual, team or organization much more than the actual error that may have occurred. An inability to see the error and/or the unwillingness to accept responsibility both impede leaders' learning and growth.

Overcoming Mistakes, Bouncing Back

What should we do when we do get tripped up by mistake?

1. *Own it:* And do it quickly. Share it with your immediate leader or manager, seek direction and share thoughts on making amends.
2. *Reflect on it:* What did you learn about yourself, others and the situation after committing the mistake?
3. *Recognize impact:* Business impact hits you first, and you will know when your errors resulted in that. However,

---

[45]McKay, Brett and Kate McKay, 'Personal Responsibility 101: Why Is It So Hard to Own Up to Our Mistakes?' *Art of Manliness (AOM)*, 18 February 2013, https://www.artofmanliness.com/articles/owning-up-to-mistakes/, accessed 30 June 2021.

small mistakes and oversights can have a more significant and long-term impact on the team and organization.

4. *Improve your ability to make decisions:* Read, learn and find out what you can do to make better decisions and what is coming in your way right now. It is very important to be aware of our shortcomings if we want to rectify them. Here, I would suggest reading the article 'Why Good Leaders Make Bad Decisions'[46] in the *Harvard Business Review*.

   The article informs us that despite high level of intelligence and best intentions, sometimes our decisions turn out to be flawed. Our vision and capabilities get distorted by emotional attachments and memories that did not serve us well. The article encourages us to question our trigger of biases, focus on identifying red flags and be more analysis driven. The authors suggest we establish a strong governance system so that many leaders get involved with the decision-making process and potentially reduce the risks of making mistakes.

5. *Get familiar with the leadership journey:* Read books, blogs and articles so you know if what you are experiencing is normal and expected, and when you should reach out for help.

6. *Find a mentor:* This is one of the mistakes I made. I have shared earlier that I lacked guidance from my family on navigating the professional and corporate world. No one had such an experience, and I struggled immensely. I did not recognize the need or possibility of a mentor's guidance until 12 years into my career, and then it played a pivotal role in my growth and success.

7. *Solicit feedback and support:* If you believe a leader's

---

[46]Campbell, Andrew, Jo Whitehead and Sydney Finkelstein, 'Why Good Leaders Make Bad Decisions,' *Harvard Business Review*, February 2009, https://hbr.org/2009/02/why-good-leaders-make-bad-decisions, accessed 30 June 2021.

journey is about going the distance alone, you are setting yourself up to fail. Open up, share, ask, *listen* and let yourself be human!

In this context, I would like to draw your attention to Jack Welch's leadership style. He encouraged people to be quick with making decisions and then be prompt enough to course correct if needed. Over-thinking can get in the way of decision-making. In 1963, his first year at GE, Welch was responsible for literally blowing up a chemical factory. Welch had been convinced that he would be fired when he would answer to Charlie Reed, an executive who was several ranks up. But Reed did not 'roast' him. Instead he asked Welch for advice on how to prevent future explosions. This restored Welch's confidence and deepened his commitment to GE. It also sowed the seeds for Welch's philosophy on encouraging and managing errors. I share his sentiment when he says, 'When people make mistakes, the last thing they need is discipline. It is time for encouragement and confidence-building. The job at this point is to restore self-confidence. I think "piling on" when someone is down is one of the worst things any of us can do.'[47]

As leaders, it is essential to be mindful of this thought. As people who will also make mistakes along the way, building the capacity to take personal responsibility will further your personal and professional journeys.

The Steve Jobs Story

Failures remind me of the life and journey of Steve Jobs. A mastermind of technological innovation and corporate vision, Jobs was responsible for making Apple the company it is today. However, his past is littered with failures, setbacks and crushing defeats. Jobs started Apple in 1976, and the company began to take off. However, after an unsuccessful product launch in 1985, Jobs was thrown out of his own company. Most ordinary people would have given up at that point, but instead, Jobs founded a new company called NeXT, which was considered unsuccessful as well, at least for a time, until it caught the eye of a struggling Apple in 1997.

Apple purchased the company and brought Jobs back into a leadership position, which he used to develop and launch Apple's breakthrough products, including the iPod, iPhone and iPad. His story shows that perseverance is everything. Because he committed himself to doing great things, Jobs was able to work past his personal and professional failures and eventually leave behind a monumental and unprecedented legacy.

---

[47]https://www.mattmcwilliams.com/jack-welch-confidence-quote/. Accessed 29 July 2021.

If you are going to take bold bets, they are going to be experiments. And if they are experiments, you do not know ahead of time if they are going to work. But a few big successes compensate for dozens and dozens of things that didn't work.

—Jeff Bezos, Amazon founder

Experiment Your Way Through

Vineet Nayar, former CEO of HCL Technologies (2007–13), is keen to frame his work at HCL as a series of experiments. Experiments go together with mistakes; in fact, he estimates that about 90 per cent of his experiments at HCL were mistakes, and only 10 per cent worked. But that does not mean they were not worth doing.

He says, 'When you experiment, you should know fully well that there's a 90 per cent probability that your hypothesis will fail. Frame your experiments in a way that you'll either prove it right or prove it wrong. The problem is companies tend to approach things as initiatives [not experiments].'

The problem with announcing a series of initiatives, he points out, is that 'people sit back and wait to judge you'. He then goes on to add something especially significant. 'If you communicate to people that you are going to experiment together, and it might fail, they will collaborate, participate and give you feedback. The moment you stand on a chair and announce an initiative, all who disagree with it will work to pull you down. You have to experiment your way through and be prepared for 90 per cent of it not working. That is where the difference between experiment and initiative lies.'

Vineet cites the example of a programme that was launched at HCL. It allowed employees to open 'trouble tickets'[48], which the management then had to solve in a limited time. When it was launched, thousands of tickets were opened. 'We started celebrating that we had captured and solved so many problems,' he recalls. 'Then a 23-year-old employee in London said: "Vineet, you are a fool. Which CEO celebrates the fact that their employees have thousands of problems?" The programme was duly changed to become preventative rather than reactive.'

---

[48]He replicated a process of customer service. Just as we call an organization for a complaint or service, a reference number/trouble ticket is created for better follow up. Vineet Nayar created a similar system to track issues raised by employees. He has always stressed that employees come before anything else.

For You to Reflect in Your Own Light

What key messages have stayed with you from the chapter?

_____

_____

_____

_____

_____

Uncover deeper sources and emotions beneath your surface attitudes. Close your eyes and take deep, slow breaths until you feel your heart beat become steady and your body relax. Then allow your mind to float back in time to the earliest memory you have of making a mistake that had negative consequences. What was the incident? What was the mistake you had committed? Who else, if anyone, was involved, and who experienced the maximum impact from the mistake? How did this experience affect you emotionally? How did it affect your feelings and attitude towards future mistakes?

_____
_____
_____
_____
_____
_____

How do you respond when someone expresses anger or disappointment over a mistake you have made? Do you become defensive, or do you feel angry and disappointed with yourself? How does your response affect your self-image?

_____
_____
_____
_____
_____

What's your immediate response to the following quote by David M. Burns: 'Aim for success, not perfection. Never give up your right to be wrong because then you will lose the ability to learn new things and move forward with your life'? What does it mean to have the 'right to be wrong?' How would (or does) hanging onto that right affect your life?

_____
_____
_____
_____
_____

What is the biggest mistake you ever made? How did it change your life, and what did you learn from that experience? If you had a chance to do it all over again, would you allow yourself to make the same mistake? If not, what different turn do you imagine your life would have taken?

_____

_____

_____

_____

_____

Do you respond differently to others' mistakes (big and small) than to your own? Yes or no, why do you think that is so? Give reasons to substantiate your answer.

_____

_____

_____

WHEN LEADERS MAKE MISTAKES
SUCCESS IS A LOUSY TEACHER. IT SEDUCES SMART PEOPLE INTO THINKING THEY CAN'T LOSE
BILL GATES
LEADERS WITHOUT CONFIDENCE - The real COST of an INTOLERANCE TOWARDS MISTAKES
I have NOT FAILED, not ONCE. I've DISCOVERED 10000 WAYS that don't WORK.
THOMAS EDISON
EMBRACE YOUR FAILURES
IF YOU ARE NOT TAKING THE RISK YOU ARE PLAYING SMALL
WHAT CAN I DO WHEN I've TRIPPED UP?
OWN IT AND DO IT QUICKLY!
REFLECT ON IT
RECOGNIZE IMPACT
IMPROVE YOUR ABILITY to MAKE DECISIONS
GET FAMILIAR WITH the LEADERSHIP JOURNEY
FIND A MENTOR
SOLICIT FEEDBACK AND SUPPORT
HOW DO I UNDERSTAND MISTAKES?
NLP
NO FAILURE FEEDBACK
FAILURE
SUCCESS
CONTEXT
BECOMING A LEADER IS SYNONYMOUS BECOMING WITH YOURSELF.
self reflections
AM I MAKING ENOUGH MISTAKES?
WHAT KIND of MISTAKES DO I FIND MYSELF MAKING?
HOW DO I RESPOND WHEN PEOPLE IN MY TEAM MAKE MISTAKES?

6

ENGAGE YOUR EMPLOYEES AS CO-CREATORS

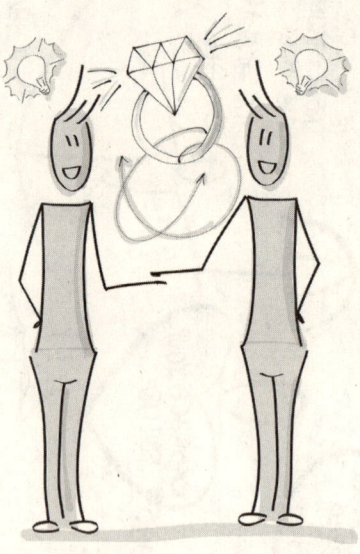

I have seen competent leaders who stood in front of a platoon, and all they saw was a platoon. But great leaders stand in front of a platoon and see it as 44 individuals, each of whom aspires, each of whom wants to live, each of whom wants to do good.

—H. Norman Schwarzkopf, Retired US Army General

So far, you are learning about yourself, trying to be self-aware and self-governing, looking for ways to use your strengths, finding and working with a mentor, and taking risks that you know will pay off eventually, even if you make a few mistakes along the way.

It is said that leaders need 'followers'. The term is a misnomer. Leaders really need co-creators of solutions, working side-by-side and using their own talents and skills to help the leader accomplish the team's shared goals and vision. For many leaders, the concept of 'different but equal' is a hard one to accept. Sure, there is a chain of command, but the more it can be minimized in business, the better served the organization will be. Employees will contribute to innovation, be engaged and motivated, and make the leader appear brighter than ever.

What I Learnt

I am fascinated by how a single idea or thought can take hold of people; how an idea can shape one's approach—to work, to life, to almost anything.

Employee Connect: The Core of Leadership

Story #16

For me, the thought about what is the key/core element of a good leadership came from a conversation I had with my leader at Spectramind in 2001. At the time, Upendra Singh was serving as Vice President (Operations), and we were winding down after a long day and a lengthier night on the rooftop of the office with chips and coffee. I cannot remember the context of the conversation. Yet, I vividly recall him saying, 'Your success in the organization is directly proportionate to the amount of time you spend with your team.'

Such a simple and unassuming statement, yet it spoke directly to me about the importance of relating to the people I lead, its link to my success and the fulfilment I seek to experience in my career. I realized the need to structure my time as a leader between task-driven and people-driven demands. Many years and many experiences have passed between that conversation and the present day, but my conviction has only become more robust—people *always* come first!

As human beings, we have a profound psychological hunger for social stimulus, contact and recognition.[49] When leaders can meet that need with authenticity and sincerity, the people who work with them feel deeply seen, understood and *engaged*. I was blessed to have had such leaders guiding the way early in my career. The fantastic thing about putting people first is that the tasks get done. As a leader, my focus is on my people, and when that gets communicated to them through actions and agendas, they are free to focus on the tasks they have.

In his book, *Love and Profit*, James A. Autry writes, 'If you do not care about people, get out of management before it gets too late.'[50]

Compassion and Care

Story #17

I remember the brutal summers of Delhi, when the temperature would touch 48 degree Celsius (118 degrees Fahrenheit). In the early days of the BPM industry, when air-conditioned cabs were still a luxury, the employees (process executives) would walk in, looking listless and apathetic. No amount of motivating, coaxing or reprimanding would get them interested in the task at hand.

---

[49]Bernie, Eric, *Transactional Analysis in Psychotherapy* (Grove Press: 1961).
[50]Autry, James A., *Love and Profit: The Art of Caring Leadership* (William Morrow Paperbacks: 1992), Page 21.

Their job was to call people in an entirely different context and help them resolve problems. This did not seem genuinely relevant to the weather-beaten executives at the time. I knew that if I wanted them to care about the people on the call, I had to care for them first. And it did not require significant thought, planning or expense. We did simple things to show we cared. On certain days, we would get Rooh Afza (a popular summer drink) for the employees at the start of the shift. They mattered; their discomfort and commitment were recognized.

As people, we all are touched when we receive care and attention—that is what builds and deepens bonds. Looking out for and responding to such real-time opportunities is what lets people know they are valued. And when people feel valued, they are available and willing to engage fully. You will notice that most of these gestures do not cost much, but they leave a lasting impression on the people who experience them. In my conversation with Sam Swaminathan, he mentioned that one's curiosity as a leader and an intent to help teammates build connected teams.

Another incident that brings a smile to my face is when we decided to leave a Post-it note and a rose on each desk with a personalized message on the launch day of a process. This created a positive buzz on the Operations floors and made our newly graduated process executives feel welcomed and emotionally connected to the larger organization.

Organizing an informal 'Gluttons Club' on Fridays at GECIS/Genpact, wherein the team members were encouraged to bring in some snacks from home, helped break the monotony and build a bond amongst the team members.

Appreciation Has a Long Shelf Life

During my discussions with Raman, I was able to better appreciate employee engagement. According to him, looking at employee engagement only for your employee's tenure was the wrong way of doing things. He remembered employees who have worked with him in Spectramind for a short year, in American Express or GE Capital for one and a half years, saying that the time they spent in the organization has been rewarding personally and professionally. Many senior and junior employees come back to say that they left because the grass was greener on the other side, but that they miss working with him, the work culture and the environment, and they want to come back. This engagement aspect is not the aspect that can be fulfilled in the tenure in which the person is your employee. It is a life-long pursuit that must be ingrained in your actions. You can become a part of your employee's life. 'At any point, up to 50 per cent of employees are at the tipping point between engaged and disenfranchised. If people really are "our greatest asset", then leaders need to put people first and profits will follow,' says Bobby Chatterjee, Senior Director, HR, Hertz.

For employees, something that their immediate manager says becomes a part of the conversations they have with their spouse, partners, mom or even friends; it becomes the organization's word. Hence, employee engagement should happen across levels and across the organization. Raman believes that employment is only the initiation of employee engagement; it is what we give to the employee and what the employee gives to the company that makes all the difference. It is a long-term relationship that you build with the employee.

However, looking at engagement as being only linked to or being impacted by attrition is a narrower view. Engagement is an umbrella that covers a multitude of tasks such as talking to your employees, listening to them, responding to what they want, getting employees to understand what our customers want and how they can be delivered. These are all components of employee engagement, and all of them must be fulfilled. However, if you choose to behave differently or start practising engagement just because there is high attrition rate or employee turnover, it is not 'engagement' in its most fundamental sense. There must be a proactive approach in your dialogue with them and in building your organization's right culture.

It is the overall 'experience' at various touchpoints that stays with your employee for life. Engagement is an opportunity for leaders to participate in their employee's life. And if you take up the challenge and make the impact, then you will be friends for life. Having said that, we should also understand that we cannot impact everybody's life. People leave and will leave because of higher aspirations, but they will at least part as friends. They will not leave with a bitter taste in their mouth.

Employee engagement is including, but not limited to, the CEO's responsibility or a specific level. Engagement needs to be a part of your organization's culture. Your ability to participate in your employee's life determines the quality of your employee engagement.

My mother always fondly remembered a sweet gesture when Raman invited his staff's families to the new Spectramind office. He gracefully touched her feet, seeking blessings for a successful launch. A leader always connects at a deeper level and inspires a larger group.

In my recent conversation with my friend, Nancy Katyal, who is an Executive Presence Coach, she made some profound comments on engaging with employees. She referred to the 'Grace-powered Leader'[51] and reinforced by stating that a great leader always conveyed messages such as:

- I am with you
- Let's go together (a co-traveller)

[51]Lawson, Steve, 'How to Become a Grace-powered Leader', *Biblical Leadership*, 31 October 2017, https://www.biblicalleadership.com/blogs/how-to-become-a-grace-powered-leader/, accessed 30 June 2021.

A great leader focuses on the 'real stuff' above superficial ways of working. They believe in 'being vs doing' and 'expression vs impression.'

At the end of the day, your team members always remember how you made them feel.

Frugal Innovation at Work

Story #18

As I reflect on Raman's perspectives, I am reminded of two memorable experiences during my stint with Wipro in 2002. Since our new campus was still being built, we did not have a large room for employee recognition sessions. The bright idea of booking a cinema hall during its off-peak hours brought a refreshing approach to employee engagement. We used the stage near the movie screen for the rewards ceremony and subsequently, played a popular Hindi comedy movie with popcorn, soft drinks and loads of laughter amongst the team members. Our clients from the UK also joined us and enjoyed the event, with team members taking turns translating the key messages from the movie!

In another case where budgets were restricted, I coordinated with a fresh coconut vendor to set up a kiosk in the ample space near the coffee area. With a few garlands and hats, and music, we recreated the Hawaiian environment, which created a unique buzz at work and people would look forward to unwinding. This low-cost engagement activity worked wonders.

Announcing an impromptu JLT (Just Like That) coffee break on a Friday afternoon with the team at a coffee shop on the work campus gave me a massive opportunity for a more in-depth and meaningful connection with my team members. We purposefully chose to speak on personal matters, particularly unique achievements such as a marathon run, volunteer work, unwinding by playing an instrument, challenges in parenting and more.

I used to write my comments on the performance dashboards (visual representation of performance data displayed on the business floors). This practice was helpful in providing encouraging feedback and recognizing good work immediately especially if the employees were on a day off or working late night when it was difficult to meet them in person.

Infosys continues to organize flash mobs and invite celebrity singers at special events as a part of employee connect initiatives.[52]

A connect at a deeper level is extremely important. Following an open-door policy, providing comfort to your people to reach you when they seek help and direction or even sharing their personal challenges, is vital for building a genuine and deeper connection. You may not have answers to all the issues; just being there for them, listening to your colleague and providing an outlet to let the steam out are helpful.

International consultant Susan Scott gives a piece of straightforward advice: 'If you want to become a great leader or a great human being, you must gain the capacity to connect with the people who are important to you at a deep level. Or lower your aim.'

I found a relationship poem in a leadership book by James Autry several years ago. Over time, I forgot almost everything else in that book, except the poem titled 'Threads'. Odd, isn't it? A poem about leadership? To be a poet of any worth, one needs to be a keen observer of people. This poem says the same is true of a good leader. To lead well is to pay attention to the clues people give us about what is going on beneath their lives' surface. It is to listen well. It is the cornerstone of any good relationship. Here is the poem:

---

[52]Chanda, Himani, 'Bonding over flash mobs. Companies focus on your dancing shoes,' *Hindustan Times*, 7 October 2016, https://www.hindustantimes.com/business-newspaper/at-workplace-fm-means-flash-mob/story-UC9qoSQMiUcWPOwSTDcQeO.html, accessed 30 June 2021.

Threads

Sometimes you just connect, like that,
no big thing maybe
but something beyond the usual business stuff.
It comes and goes quickly
so you have to pay attention,
A change in the eyes
When you ask about the family,
a pain flickering behind the statistics
about a boy and a girl in school,
or about seeing them every other Sunday.
An older guy talks about his bride,
A little affection. After twenty-five years.
A hot-eyed achiever laughs before you want him to.
Someone tells about his wife's job
or why she quit working to stay home.
An older joker needs another laugh on the way to retirement.
A woman says she spends a lot of her salary on an au pair*
and a good one is hard to find
but it is worth it because there is nothing more important
than the baby.
Listen.
In every office you hear the threads
of love and joy and fear and guilt,
the cries for celebration and reassurance,
and somehow you know that connecting those threads
is what you are supposed to do,
and business just takes care of itself.[53]

*House help, Nanny

---

[53]Autry, James A., *Love and Profit: The Art of Caring Leadership* (Avon Books; Reprint edition, 1992), Page 26. Quoted in Finzel, Hans, *The Top Ten Mistakes Leaders Make* (David C. Cook: 2007).

Yes, connecting those threads is what you're supposed to do. Imagine, if we all listened well, whether we are a leader or not, how different things would be!

What are the threads you see in the relationships around you? What are they leading you to do? In the new, supercharged, superfast, super-competitive economy, we need customers to love our brands, love our products and advocate for our companies. Surely, customer love must start with employee love?

Timely Recognition: The Hallmark of a Leader

Story #19

I have an experience to share on timely recognition, which results in a better engagement with employees. This was way back in 2000, when I managed a technical support team for a global computer giant, Dell. Internet connections were not very stable then, and our team's typing skills required a lot of improvement. I had set up a goal of 50 emails a day, and we celebrated the achievers through loud cheers and clapping on the business floor.

Since the CEO's office was on the same floor, whenever Raman, our CEO, heard the cheer, he would step out and ask me who the achievers were and then shake hands with them. This continued for a few days until, one day, Raman asked me to step aside and whispered in my ear, 'Is this recognition accompanied by some tangibles?' I shared my concerns around a 'recognition policy' not being in place yet (this was the beginning of our operations) and limited budgets. Raman was quick to respond and shared some words of wisdom. He said that timely recognition with some tangibles, even though of a small value, is far more impactful than a more considerable recognition that gets delayed by weeks.

With a smile on his face, he prompted me to organize some

Indian sweets for the employees and send a few to his office! This advice has stayed well with me for all these years, and I always carry a few blank greeting cards with me in my bag for 'on-the-spot' recognition wherever I see excellent customer service behaviour in action. Instant gratification has its own merits.

This further reminds me of another great practice followed by a GE company during a project stint in Orlando, US, many years ago. A group of HR and business leaders would walk on the operations floor and hand over recognition (books, gift vouchers, etc.) to a high performer. This reward was aptly branded as 'You've Been Spotted'!

Family events and floor walks by the leadership, especially during night shifts, helped build a deeper connection with the associates, who felt that they did not have access or visibility with the senior leaders. Floor walks, town-hall sessions and skip-level interactions, including coffee with the leader, have helped build a positive employee experience.

With increased expectations for personalized experiences that follow consumer trends and a tight job market, there is a growing need for companies to stay competitive by creating better employee experiences. Organizations that provide a more flexible and personalized approach to work and career development will continue to lead the way and set the bar for how best to retain and grow talent.

According to research conducted by YouEarnedIt[54] (now branded as Kazoo), employee experience consists of four key pillars:

- *Connection*: Feeling engaged with your manager, colleagues, company and community.
- *Meaning*: Knowing that your job and your company has

---

[54]'YouEarnedIt Defines Employee Experience with New Market Research Report', 9 August 2017, https://www.prweb.com/releases/2017/08/prweb14585249.htm, accessed 10 July 2021.

relevance and purpose.

- *Impact:* Understanding how the work you do affects your colleagues and your company for the better.
- *Appreciation:* Being recognized and acknowledged for your contributions.

The foundation of positive work experience is company culture. According to Ingersoll Rand, a diversified industrial manufacturer with close to 46,000 employees and revenue of $14.6 billion, it is a 'winning culture'.[55] For the company, this attitude is a differentiator in the marketplace.

'We asked everyone to think about how we work,' says Michelle Murphy, vice president of diversity and inclusion and global talent acquisition.[56] He continues by saying, 'How can we structure it? Will we have teams with part-time workers? Will we have people on flexible schedules? The point is that we need to expand our vision of how we get the work done.'

Introducing flexible work schedules and encouraging coaching and mentoring services from their veteran/retired resources are among the best ways to utilize the skills of the retired resources. This enables the company and culture to retain those years of knowledge and experience.

Another measure of autonomy, which is a valued trait of good work experience, is the ability to determine employee career paths. While this is especially important to attract and retain millennials, the concept holds true for all age groups. The programme called 'Career Progress' at Ingersoll Rand looks at critical roles across every function throughout the organization and creates a successful senior role profile. Engaged employees

---

[55]Selko, Adrienne, 'It's Not a Job, It's an Employee Experience,' *Industry Week*, 17 December 2018, https://www.industryweek.com/talent/article/22026847/its-not-a-job-its-an-employee-experience, accessed 12 July 2021.
[56]Ibid.

build better, healthier and more resilient organizations. They do this in three ways:

1. By making better decisions because they understand more about the organization, its customers and the context they are operating in.
2. By being more productive because they like or love what they are doing. They waste less time and get less distracted by things that do not further their mission or goals.
3. By innovating more because they sincerely want the organization to succeed.

Tata Group's former chairman, Ratan Tata, is known for his humility and deep engagement with his employees, and there are countless examples that illustrate that. He started out by working as a blue-collar employee for Tata Steel. He personally visited the families of the 80 employees who were affected by the 26/11 terrorist attacks at the Taj hotel in Mumbai in 2008. He remembers almost everyone by their first names. He is loved by all who know him and, as a leader, he has taken the concept of employee engagement to an entirely different level.

The COVID-19 Challenge

From communicating regularly through virtual town halls to introducing programmes that focus on employees' well-being, companies have leveraged all possible ways to keep employees socially connected as they work from home—the new normal in the post-COVID-19 world. It is also vital for companies to understand the stress employees are going through during this time; hence, it is essential to be compassionate as an organization and build platforms where employees can discuss the issues they are dealing with. The Tata Group of companies invests in organizing webinars, wherein they invite guest speakers from across the globe to talk about managing under uncertain times, stress management and more. A regular session on fitness conducted by an employee is gaining a lot of attention and appreciation.

Companies are finding innovative ways of using technology to connect people even when they are physically distanced. Several companies are organizing contests, challenges and hackathons with the help of various tech collaboration tools to share real-time actionable ideas for businesses to battle and recover from the aftermaths of COVID-19.

Infosys regularly engages employees through work from home moments-related videos, special occasion interviews such as on Mother's Day or diversity- and inclusivity-associated videos. These videos and related posts of teams working across the globe are consistently posted on various social media channels.[57]

Such initiatives help in bringing employees together and foster innovation. Technology is also being leveraged to facilitate seamless collaboration between the frontline staff and customers. Town halls, team meetings, new business pitches and even break-time shenanigans are being conducted virtually to break the monotony of working alone and working remotely.

---

[57]'Employee engagement for remote work: A redefined approach for the new normal,' *Infosys BPM*, https://www.infosysbpm.com/blogs/human-resource-outsourcing/employee-engagement-for-remote-work-a-redefined-approach-for-the-new-normal.html, accessed 30 June 2021.

Diving Deep: Research Insights

I slept and dreamt that life was joy. I awoke and saw that life was service. I acted and behold, service was joy.

—Rabindranath Tagore,
Noble laureate and spiritual leader

Knowing what causes disengagement from the role, the manager and/or the organization is an essential first step in building a plan on staying engaged and putting engagement on your team's agenda. Many theories attempt to explain what motivates employees and keeps them engaged at work. Mrinalini finds Hackman and Oldham's job characteristics theory of employee motivation[58] particularly apt. It proposes that a person is likely to be engaged and motivated at work if they can:

(a) Make meaning of their work and see its relevance to a larger whole,

---

[58]'Employee Motivation Theories,' Your Knowledge, https://www.yourcoach.be/en/employee-motivation-theories/hackman-oldham-job-characteristics-model.php, accessed 30 June 2021.

(b) Exercise enough responsibility and power to make an impact,

(c) Have a sense of their prospects and growth option, and

(d) Feel recognized and valued.

In the absence of any of the above factors, an employee can feel 'not engaged' with their work, which means they are only physically present. Emotionally or psychologically, they have 'checked out' and might move through their workday as if sleepwalking and *putting time, but not passion* into their work. John Wooden, a legendary US basketball player and coach said 'never mistake activity for achievement'.

A Gallup report on global employee engagement reveals that the employee engagement decreased globally by two percentage points, from 22 per cent in 2019 to 20 per cent in 2020.[59] Leaders will need to address this decline and its business impact on workplace culture, employee retention and performance.

Conventional thought on leadership and employee engagement says that an engaged employee is the one who is committed to his *organization and its vision.* There is, however, another line of thinking that might actually be more relevant for Gen X and the millennial population, which forms a much more significant percentage of the workforce, especially in the BPM industry. This approach suggests that the employee can just as quickly be committed to their own vision if it aligns with that of the organization in short- to mid-term.[60]

---

[59]State of the Global Workplace, https://www.gallup.com/workplace/349484/state-of-the-global-workplace.aspx, accessed 10 July 2021.

[60]Liz Ryan in her article on Forbes.com says,

Why do employees have to be engaged with the company mission? They may have their own mission. They may be working to save money for a house, or to get enough great resume fodder to move to Iceland and start a business there. That is their passion. They could

Engagement and disengagement exist on a spectrum from 'actively engaged' to 'actively disengaged' with shades and overlaps in between. The 'actively disengaged' employee is often the one we see as the 'troublemaker'. These employees act out their unhappiness, often disrupt productivity and undermine what their engaged co-workers are trying to accomplish. While this category may seem the most toxic, in reality, it is the large portion of 'disengaged' employees that presents the more significant problem. It is the 'quietly-present-but-mentally-checked-out' workforce that slowly drains the vitality of an organization.

The Culture of Engagement

So, how does a leader go about creating an engaged workforce? Even the best-intentioned leaders will struggle with getting to know *all* their people well enough to tell what they will be engaged by. An interesting alternative is for the leader to *model* engagement, talk about how you keep yourself engaged and encourage others to seek out that which engages them. Suddenly, you have a team that takes ownership of their engagement and approaches you for guidance and conversations rather than a group of people you must *carry*, take ownership of, satisfy and keep engaged! Your job is to *put engagement on the agenda* and then provide the support to see it happen.

Recognizing that there is a difference between compliance and commitment helped the CEO of Johnsonville Sausage, Ralph

---

not care less about the company's mission, and really, why should they? The job is a means to an end for them. That is okay! Let us be honest—paying people to come to work is a means to an end for the company, too.

(Ryan, Liz, 'What Does "Employee Engagement" Mean?' *Forbes*, 4 April 2015, http://www.forbes.com/sites/lizryan/2015/04/04/what-does-employee-engagement-mean/, accessed 30 June 2021.

Stayer, turn his company around. According to him, to change the engagement level amongst employees, one has to change their own leadership behaviour first. If an engaged workforce and great performance are what leaders desire, they cannot merely demand more engagement and better performance. They cannot just stand on the sidelines and criticize. Ask yourself: when was the last time I felt genuinely alive at work? When was the last time I was so engaged in my work that I lost track of time? When did I last, in the words of psychologist Mihaly Csikszentmihalyi, experience 'flow'[61]?

If the answer is more than a few days or a few weeks ago, or if you find yourself saying, 'I can't *remember* when I last felt like that', then this is a good chapter for you to spend some time on. While there is no expected range of answers to these questions, it is crucial to knowing how often you feel *engaged* at work and what creates that feeling for you.

The first step, of course, is to assess whether *you* are genuinely engaged with your work. If you feel 'used up', 'burnt out', 'drained' or 'fatigued' consistently, then engagement has to begin with you. If you find your engagement level flagging, this might be an excellent time to identify what's amiss and take action to bring yourself back to your work—wholeheartedly.

An engaged leader fosters engagement in his team, and this has been the case for me personally. I recognize that having a sense of purpose and positively influencing lives provide a sense of direction to my team. And feeling valued and recognized in the organizations I have worked for helps me have a deep and sustainable understanding of engagement. The satisfaction of watching initiatives see the light of day, despite challenges and setbacks, are other things that give me the drive to bring my

---

[61]Csikszentmihalyi, Mihaly, *Flow: The Psychology of Optimal Experience* (Harper & Row: 1990).

whole self to work. Contrary to popular belief, facing challenges and seeing them through are great ways to feel engaged and involved in your work. Often, an extremely stable environment can also disengage people and promote boredom and monotony. According to Csikszentmihalyi, the optimal functioning zone, which is where 'flow'[62] occurs, is between the point of anxiety and boredom. This point varies from person to person.

A leader's task is to create a climate that enables employees to unleash their true potential by identifying opportunities, having regular contact points with the team, encouraging thinking and directing action around employee engagement. Sometimes, people perform better in another function or with another client or process, and a good leader develops the skills to spot that and allow it to happen. The BPM industry grew so fast that people's job placements became driven by time rather than their innate inclinations. This now has a chance of finding balance.

It is the role of mentors and leaders to develop the foresight to see their people's potential and help them select and walk the path of their growth and success. I have immensely benefitted from my mentors' foresight and guidance on my strengths and career choices. And today, I want to do that for those whom I meet.

In order to look ahead, see people for who they are and who they can be and then give them the space to develop themselves— that is the hallmark of a good leader.

At Infosys, we were able to make an incredibly positive connection with our associates through an innovative mentoring programme called 'Guru Cool'. The concept was to connect a leader with a group of newly joined associates. A leader would meet up once a month with an identified group, and share their personal journey and provide them with the much-needed

---

[62]Ibid.

information on various policies and career advice. In the last 10 years since it's inception in 2011, employee retention has moved up by 400 per cent through this initiative![63]

Organizations spend a great deal of time and money, ensuring they have the right policies, processes and structures in place. But without actively engaged employees, the best systems will still underperform. Leaders often expect employees to display ownership and walk the extra mile, which happens only when they are well and truly engaged. Research shows that employee engagement does not just impact bottom-line results, it *drives* results!

The concept of engagement can be 'fuzzy' or 'messy' depending on how you see it because it brings us face to face with

---

[63]This information came up during my discussion with Clifford M. Pai, Vice President and Head of employee relations at Infosys BPM.

everyone's subjectivity and uniqueness—what deeply engages one employee may have no meaning for another. So, while there may be broad, over-the-counter 'engagement exercises' that the organization initiates, the leader's job is to breathe life into them—to make them relevant to their people. And the best place to start is to take stock of your own degree of engagement in the organization.

The American multinational technology company Nvidia Corporation designs graphics processing units for gaming and professional markets as well as system on chip units for mobile computing and automotive industries. While the general assumption is that high-tech companies are turning themselves inside out to attract and retain millennials, Nvidia surveys its entire workforce to tailor benefits. A good example is a service they offer employees nearing retirement called CareCounsel, which can help plan for Medicare options. They also have a high-level concierge who can seek out medical care that benefits older employees.[64]

Millennials are not ignored. In fact, the company addresses one of this segment's most significant concern: student debt. Employees can get $6,000 of their debt paid yearly (up to $30,000). And for employees at the family stage, the company pays for in vitro fertilization and adoption. Other benefits include onsite services, such as mobile health clinics, car maintenance, and even laundry services!

'One of the things that continue to impress me over the 14 years I have been here [is that] we provide the same level of benefits and services to everyone,' Beau Davidson, the vice president of employee experience, says adding, 'The CEO has no special perks. Segregating one group from another is detrimental. We are all treated equally, and when everyone is part of the same program, it creates an environment where we are working toward the greater benefit of everyone.'[65]

In 2018, this factor has led to a turnover rate of less than 5 per cent at Nvidia—a meagre number for Silicon Valley.

IBM's Employee Experience

Information technology giant IBM undertook an effort to co-create its 'Employee Experience' (EX) with employees, bringing employees into the EX design process[66] and iterating EX to ensure the company is meeting their needs. An onboarding process that includes providing new employees with the tools and information

---

[64]Selko, Adrienne, 'It's Not a Job, It's an Employee Experience,' *Industry Week*, 17 December 2018, https://www.industryweek.com/talent/article/22026847/its-not-a-job-its-an-employee-experience, accessed 30 June 2021.

[65]Ibid.

[66]Lisa Burrell, 'Co-Creating the Employee Experience,' *Harvard Business Review*, March–April 2018, https://hbr.org/2018/03/co-creating-the-employee-experience, accessed 30 June 2021.

they need, a further Netflix-like digital training and development programme, and a brand-new crowdsourced performance review process are among the changes the company has implemented.

Starbucks's Anti-bias Programme

In May 2018, Starbucks closed its stores throughout the US and engaged all 175,000 employees in a four-hour anti-bias training session. The move was prompted by two African-American men's wrongful arrest by police, who had been summoned by a Starbucks manager. The training was intended to make employees more aware of unconscious discrimination, align everyone around and affirm its commitment to diversity and service. The priority Starbucks placed on the training, and its nature and scope, which included videos by company leaders and prominent cultural figures, facilitated discussions and problem-solving scenarios. This represents a best-in-class approach to employee training.

The most recent incident of George Floyd, an African-American man killed by the police during an arrest in Minneapolis, Minnesota, had shaken the entire world on 25 May 2020.[67] It sparked debates around lack of empathy, disrespecting a diverse nation's values, the need to continue raising our voice against such despicable acts and make amendments by relooking at the law and related policies. Several organizations have supported the change and have started amplifying their communication in solidarity and upholding their values.

Hilton's Employee Hospitality

During 2017–18, Hilton Hotels made an investment in EX's often-overlooked aspects by upgrading its employee spaces, including

---

[67]'How George Floyd Was Killed in Police Custody,' *The New York Times*, 31 May 2020, https://www.nytimes.com/2020/05/31/us/george-floyd-investigation.html, accessed 30 June 2021.

cafeterias and locker rooms. This is one of the many significant moves the company took to improve EX and to reflect its understanding that it can't achieve its mission of becoming 'the most hospitable company in the world' if it's not hospitable to its employees.

Indigo's Flight to Triumph

Aditya Ghosh, former CEO of the low-cost Indian airline, Indigo, is the leader behind IndiGo's flight to triumph. While the industry was facing retrenchments and salary delays in 2017, IndiGo has never retrenched its staff. He said, 'We have never delayed the salaries even by an hour.'[68]

Aditya cites the example of Sachin Tendulkar to drive home the point that appreciation is equally important as the pay. Sachin is supposed to play hard. After all, he earns a hefty amount of money through match fees and endorsements and has millions of fans across the world. Yet, every time he scores a six, or hits a century, the audience claps and cheers for him. Why? The reason is simple—we reward the cricketer not only by money but also by recognizing his efforts. The respect given to him encourages him to hit another six and win the match for India.

Ghosh says that each one of 'their total 14,000 people employed is playing in the middle of the pitch, who put their lives in danger by hanging themselves in the middle of the air, leaving their personal responsibilities besides the professional requirements'[69].

Here are some nuggets of wisdom from leaders I engaged with during the research work of this book. Gopal Devanahalli, my former leader at Infosys and now the CEO of Manipal Education Americas, shares these pointers:

---

[68]Chandna, Himani, 'Aditya Ghosh: A leader behind IndiGo's flight to triumph,' *BW People.in*, 21 June 2017, http://bwpeople.businessworld.in/article/Aditya-Gosh-A-leader-behind-IndiGo-s-flight-triumph-/21-06-2017-120556/, accessed 30 June 2021.
[69]Ibid.

- Engage regularly with your teams.
- Initiate calendar-based reviews. Always be available for support.
- Engage in solution-oriented conversations to build a positive work culture.
- Regular skip-level meetings help a leader get a pulse on the work environment.

I believe that employee engagement is an investment that every organization needs to make to stay in business. When people are financially invested, they want a financial return, however when people are emotionally invested, they stretch to contribute and make a difference. And that's the essence and glue to keep them in an organization.

—Clifford M. Pai, VP, H.R. Head. APAC & EMEA and Global Head—Employee Relations, Infosys BPM

For You to Reflect in Your Own Light

What key messages have stayed with you from the chapter?

_____
_____
_____
_____
_____
_____

When was the last time you were in the 'flow' state at work? What was it like? How can you create more such flow states for yourself?

_____
_____
_____
_____
_____

As you reflect upon turning your employees/team members into co-creators, I invite you to think of a couple of things you can do to recognize them authentically. What can you do to show more compassion and care? (Read Kim Scott's *Radical Candor*[70] to understand how to care genuinely.)

_____
_____
_____
_____
_____

How can you improve your team's 'overall experience' with you and within the organization? Think of small steps you can take in that direction. (Remember my story of bringing Rooh Afza in the summers of Delhi and the JLT coffee breaks?)

_____
_____
_____
_____
_____

As you read the poem 'Threads' (page 106), think about the threads you see in the relationships around you? What are they leading you to do?

_____
_____
_____
_____

[70]Scott, Kim, *Radical Candor: Be a Kick-Ass Boss Without Losing Your Humanity.* (St. Martin's Press: 2017).

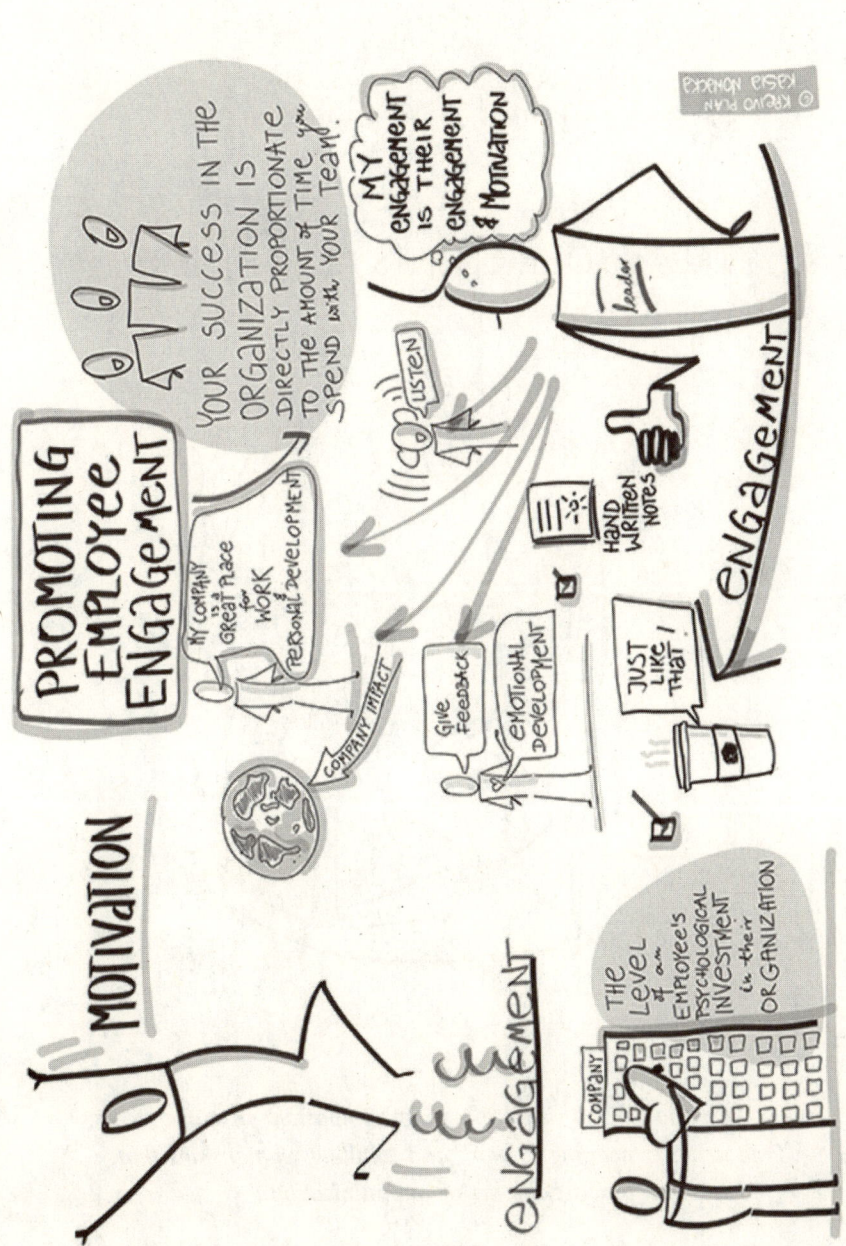

7

TREAT YOUR CLIENTS AS PARTNERS

There may be no single thing more important in our efforts to achieve meaningful work and fulfilling relationships than to learn to practise the art of communication.

—Max De Pree, American businessman and author

I began discussing relationships a while back when I suggested that good leaders work best when they have mentors to help improve their interactions and decisions. I also mentioned that the best way to work with team members is to treat them as co-creators of project solutions. Everyone has a job to do, and although there is a chain of command, it should not be needed if leaders and co-creators respect each other and share the risks and rewards of getting things done in innovative ways.

There is another relationship that is particularly important in organizations, and that is the relationship the organization has with its clients. Like employees, clients too want to be considered partners with the organization that serves them. If leaders and their companies can treat clients as partners, both will be successful in achieving a win-win relationship.

What I Learnt

Managing client relations is an integral and often challenging part of a leader's work. This is not because there is something inherently problematic about *this* relationship; it is because, as human beings, we often struggle with *most* relationships.

Story #20

One of the most challenging experiences of managing clients was when I first joined Infosys in 2006. I was responsible for managing the accounts of several clients who had placed vendor managers on location. Entering a new space and taking on the responsibility of renegotiating established expectations and dynamics can be challenging. But it can also be an invaluable learning experience. Soon, I realized that there was some disconnect between what the sales team had committed and what we were capable of delivering. Having the vendor managers watch for slip-ups and loopholes did not help. They performed a quality control function and were responsible for assessing our capabilities. As you can imagine, this did not put me in a comfortable position. I was now accountable for realigning the previously set *unrealistic* expectations while demonstrating result orientation and capability from the word 'go'!

The concept of placing vendor managers on-site was new at the time but is a common practice today. Also, in the early days of outsourcing, clients were extra careful to protect their offshore interests. Given this context and the associated pressures, the situation could have very quickly become adversarial. Luckily, I was aware that this was a path to inevitable disaster. I decided to focus my energies into bringing them on board as allies and sharing the credit with them for even small successes.

Align Your Goals with Those of the Customers

A series of casual conversations over smokes and coffee was instrumental in gaining my client's confidence and creating buy-in. It was essential to buy time to be able to deliver on some of the over-committed projects.

In this case, the clients to be *managed* were the vendor managers, and engaging in adversarial exchanges with them would have resulted in a further loss of the freedom required; in fact, we would have invited constant interference for ourselves! The moment I was able to convince the client-vendor manager that we were working towards the same goals and focus his attention on the final result, I was able to create an environment of patience, tolerance and trust. This worked mainly for the days when things didn't move according to plan. What helped build trust and achieve better alignment was an agreement to connect every Friday over a long call, which began with discussions on the weather and sports and lead to the wins and issues on the business front.

Build a Relationship of Trust

In the above context, equally important was an agreement with the vendor manager that he would get to know of any operational issues directly from me rather than through different sources. This worked for us as it lead to better communication and less misunderstanding. He understood that there would be issues common in any large-scale ramp up and clearly wanted to be on top of the problem and work with me to resolve it. To cut a long story short, he wanted me to be candid and honest rather than beating around the bush.

This experience had me reflecting on what 'client management' really means. The word 'manage' conjures up images of just about making it through—especially with relationships. I prefer looking at it as a process of building relationships—genuine, heartfelt relationships that are deeply embedded in the professional context but still have a personal contact element. An honest and sincere relationship would also mean sharing your vulnerabilities.

During my discussions with Gopal, my former leader at Infosys, some additional insights came to the surface. With regard to client engagement, he has always believed in creating a call plan before engaging with his clients. This plan would include key objectives as well as the value adds being envisioned for the client. Based on his experience of heading an extensive customer service practice at Infosys BPM, Gopal recommends the following:

- Build a complete alignment with the client.
- Genuinely try to understand the client's business—the industry, business model, how they build their revenues, etc.
- Be extremely responsive and professional in your dealings with the client.
- Be curious, look out for opportunities to do more via innovation and process improvements.

In a highly recommended book, *Clients for Life,* authors Andrew Sobel and Jagdish Sheth provide profound trust messages.[71]

When a client trusts her professional adviser, several positive things happen. When you suggest additional work to your client, she believes you are proposing the work because you honestly think it will help her, not because you need more business. Your client will be willing to buy services from you that extend beyond your core expertise. If you make an honest mistake or slip-up in some way, your client will most likely forgive you. You will work with your client on a more informal basis, leading to a more open and creative process.

Your client will believe that your words are backed with integrity, data and that your 'only' agenda is to help solve her problem. Trust, in other words, is a professional's most potent ally. Trust is worth a fortune!

Customer Needs are Paramount

Steve Jobs once made a highly impactful statement in this regard, and I quote, 'Get closer than ever to your customers. So close that you tell them what they need well before they realize it themselves.'

During my conversations with Raman, I received valuable insights on this subject. In his opinion, client management is a little fuzzy world to understand. On the one hand, the client is always right and pays our salaries, and on another, we are in business to make profits; hence, we cannot agree to everything they demand without any pay raise. The most critical element in managing your clients is to understand what they need.

---

[71]Sobel, Andrew and Jagdish Sheth, *Clients for Life: Evolving from an Expert-for-Hire to an Extraordinary Adviser* (Simon & Schuster: 2002).

Making Sincere Efforts in Understanding Client Needs

Story #21

Raman was reminded of an experience he had while working in an organization that had two different clients. There was a 20-minute hold time of a customer service call for one of the clients, and in the case of another premier client, if it took more than two rings to answer a call, we were questioning the process. Customer service for them was saying that the customer's call must be answered in two rings.

Raman's team decided to improve the previous client's experience by reducing the 'average speed service'. He hired more people, increased the seats and dramatically brought down the call waiting time. Later, when he went to the quarterly review meeting with the client, he thought we would get a pat on our backs for having reduced the call waiting time. To his surprise, they beat us up, saying that they wanted that hold time because it gave the service agent a chance to refer to the manuals and provide correct solutions. Raman realized that he had not understood his client's need. He never asked what good customer service meant to them.

One company is delighted with an average waiting time of 20 minutes, and the other will not let it be more than 20 seconds. This shows us that our clients decide how they want to be positioned and what the requirements would mean to them.

Raman continued by saying that firms must cater to the client's needs while managing them, understand what is crucial for them, and then monitor whether one is improving or declining.

Unfortunately, many of us have learned to create review 'dashboards', but we measure and project generic elements in our reports. Dashboards should be based on the client's needs.

In the early days of outsourcing, clients strategically looked at ways to not send work to India. There was a criterion given to us, such as error rate percentages that had to be met if we wanted to receive work. However, it was found that the same processes functioning in their home grounds did not match the criterion either. While managing clients, you should also monitor the baselines being set for you and whether they are realistic or not. Managing clients means understanding their needs, asking the right questions to confirm our understanding and constant monitoring to ensure success. The idea of relating well has teeth only when we focus on building the skills that allow us to contact and connect well with people. And what are those skills? Let's look at them here:

1. Speak Clearly and Transparently

We often read that it is essential to be on the same page with the client regarding expectations—outcomes, timelines and resource availability. Excellent and clear communication is at the core of this requirement , not just verbal but non-verbal and tonal too. So, it goes without saying that if you want to improve your capacity to meet as well as exceed client expectations, start developing your ability to communicate well. Ask incisive and relevant questions, paraphrase to ensure understanding.

Being able to speak directly and transparently requires other skills to be mastered. Bringing your most confident (but not arrogant or overbearing) self, speaking straight (but without being brash or rude) and limiting scope (without sounding reluctant or underselling) can seem like contradictions. I can only imagine how tough it must be for new leaders to negotiate these aspects in quickly changing environments. But here as well, mastering communication skills plays a significant role. Taking the time to assess your own style of communication, its impact, asking for feedback, being in learning spaces and applying those learnings go a long way in making client relationship management more manageable and productive.

The importance of excellent and clear communication cannot be stressed enough in situations where things go wrong. Taking the right amount of responsibility while accounting for all the practical realities around the problem becomes much more comfortable when the leader can put things across crisply, with authenticity and congruence in words and non-verbal cues.

In my personal experience, seeking clarity if you cannot understand the other person's views or perspectives indicates that you have been interested in the conversation and wish to contribute and respond accordingly. Paraphrasing further helps bring clarity and leaves no room for ambiguity. Being straightforward and polite has served me well.

2. Reflect on Your Actions

We need to reflect and develop our capacity for self-awareness. When we relate to people, we connect to a frame of reference that is unique to us. We think, feel and act in ways that are consistent with that frame of reference. Reflecting on your thoughts, feelings and actions will help you be more aware of your frame of reference. For example, if you find yourself regularly over-committing to clients, it might be a good idea to reflect on what you are thinking and feeling when you are in that situation. You might hear your own thoughts and realize that you often think you should accept the client's requests for various reasons. Ideas could range from thinking that 'the customer is always the king, and I have to listen', to 'it's rude to say no', to the fear that it might adversely affect your career.

This process takes time but can be rewarding, especially if you also seek feedback from others on how they see you from the outside. Reflecting on your motivations can help you decide if you need to make some changes and what they might be. Additionally, being aware of what makes you do things such as overcommitting can help you plan for the next time you are seated across a client at a negotiating table.

3. Build and Nurture Your Goodwill

Often, we look at what we can do in a situation with a client only once we have hit the crisis point. By then, it is too late to build anything, and the leader's focus is on firefighting and just managing the situation the best that they can. Think of it as a safety net—you would not start putting it up after a crisis has occurred, would you? You need to have that net up, tried and tested well before you need to actually use it.

In client relationships, that safety net is the trust and goodwill you had built-in when you *were not* in crisis. This is not to be understood as a manipulative action, but rather a practical understanding of the fact that people would respond to you when you have taken the time to build a connection. You can only lean on a relationship if you have strengthened it in advance, or else, it will break under the pressure of the 'crisis' and its demands.

Building relationships doesn't have to be another *task* you have to get through. Simple gestures that are heartfelt help us connect meaningfully with other people.

In my recent trip to the US, I carried a few packets of *chivda* (a local snack made of rice) with me to courier to my erstwhile client, who lived in another state. The whole effort cost me a few minutes in visiting FedEx and some $10, but it sent a strong message and strengthened an old bond.

Ensuring that you make time to have catch-up sessions with clients regularly helps build this trust, goodwill and understanding. Make this a regular calendar event to ensure you have regularity, frequency and consistency.

Take advantage of the technology advances, wherein the data access, speed and access to video conferencing apps, virtual meetings and catch-up sessions have become so easy and frequent. I feel so connected and bonded with my clients, including the ones who have hung their boots and have rich experiences and exciting stories to share.

4. Invest in Understanding Client's Core Business

Ensure you take the time to understand the client's core business. Then you come across as an expert. Clients like to interact with knowledgeable people. Taking time to do this makes an impact, and the conversation becomes intelligent and productive. Make efforts to develop in-depth domain knowledge on the business you are working in. Do not jump to different organizations for small salary hikes. Instead, focus on acquiring expertise in the chosen area and move only once the learning ceases in the current organization. Until you have learnt enough about the client's business and earned their confidence, it's a good idea to hold off on suggesting process changes.

Another aspect of relationship building that I have found immensely helpful is developing the ability to create a delicate balance between the client's interest and your organization's interest. While we work for the client and build a healthy relationship, we must always keep our organization's interests in mind. The balance here is delicate but critical. Clients appreciate it when you always keep their interests in mind. Yet, dropping the ball on organizational concerns and goals can jeopardize the very reason you are there.

I recall a discussion with a colleague at Infosys, who wanted my team to help his team members improve their client communication skills. During a detailed conversation with this colleague, the team did not require communication skills the way we all understand them. From the client feedback, we realized that the client was quite happy with the team and had no language issues.

However, the client found a few areas of improvement. These included the team's inability to strike curious conversations with the on-site (client) teams. They strictly focused on their existing goals and structured way of working.

By having curious conversations and engaging well with the on-site teams, the Infosys project team could have identified new business opportunities. Failure to identify new support areas while at the on-site location turned expensive for the organization. It was clearly a lost opportunity to make significant revenues.

Beware of Misleading Assumptions

Story #22

I remember an incident from the time I was working with GE. We were trained by a domain specialist who had travelled to India from the US. The trainer was a lovely woman, who went out of her way to ensure that we understood what was expected of us. At the end of the training sessions, I took the whole team and the trainer out for a luncheon as a token of my gratitude. We went to an upmarket gourmet restaurant in a five-star hotel in Delhi which charged the company Amex card for ₹11,000 (close to $250)—a whopping amount for 1989! I was pretty pleased with the training and the way I handled the client afterwards. That was until I found out that the trainer, while being wonderful to us, was a junior person, and charging the company card to take her out might not be looked upon as favourably as I imagined.

Thankfully, sharing the details with my manager and clarifying my reasons were enough to take care of this potential faux pas. But it got me thinking—what would have happened if instead of including an extra person, I had inadvertently excluded someone I *should* have invited? Just as this was possible, so was the reverse. I consequently made sure to consistently connect with my counterpart in other countries, iron out the work details, understand their realities and structures of hierarchy, etc. Sometimes, such oversights can cause a misunderstanding that adversely affects work and productivity.

Comfort in Your Identity

Story #23

Being comfortable in your own identity—cultural, national, etc.—is particularly important. I remember an incident when, early on in my career, I was responsible for taking a prospective client from the UK for a tour around our newly constructed facility. The visit fell just before 15 August, our Independence Day. I thought it would be a good idea to show the enthusiastically decorated production bays to the clients. The client asked me, 'Who was India celebrating Independence from?' I will never know if this was out of ignorance or guile; I smiled in response. A moment that could have quickly created animosity was evaded because I did not see the need to take offence to the comment. Sometimes, the best thing we can do is smile and allow people to become aware of their statement's gracelessness in due course of time.

This, of course, occurred many years ago. Clients are much more aware and sensitive today about the cultures they work with. However, some of the biases are deep-rooted. You are likely to come across at least a handful of people who will present aggravations like this during your career. For leaders at all levels, it is essential to assess the gravity and extent of the situation before responding—sometimes, a smile and sidestepping are enough. However, sometimes, this might not be a client that your organization chooses to associate with and sharing with senior leaders will help you decide which course of action to adopt.

At the same time, I find great value in making an effort to get to know the culture one interacts with. Practising and honing your conversational skills, in general, is a great idea. It has come in very handy when I have had to break the ice with a new or prospective client. Whether you talk about the weather, sports, food, art or cinema does not usually matter. What matters is that you have made an effort to familiarize yourself with the client's culture and are willing to engage on comfortable topics. However, staying away from political and religious and faith-related discussions is recommended as that can get tricky very quickly.

Your Employees Are Your Internal Customers

I have often felt that though we cognitively know that our employees are our customers as well, in practice this gets missed out. For an organization to function with agility, there must be a high degree of internal alignment. This is where I feel young leaders can create an edge for themselves early in their career. Developing and managing relationships with various process owners (i.e. recruitment lead, training lead, etc.) is advisable as it eases the process of replacing resources—a common challenge in most organizations and in the BPM space.

Your colleagues at work who help you with recruitment, logistics, facilities, finance, etc., are 'enabling' you to do your job better. Treating them as your internal customers and recognizing their efforts help in executing successful projects, client interactions, and building trust and great teamwork.

At Wipro, I recall evolving a fantastic working relationship with a colleague, Ajoy Menon, who belonged to the IT business and was also responsible for client relationship with the BPM business. I was managing an insurance client called Friends Provident and Ajoy was responsible for the relationship with Friends Provident on the matters of IT business as well as the BPM business. A common relationship leader is the sole point of contact for a client, thus the communication is direct and precise. In the first meeting with employees of the newly acquired Spectramind, he was upfront and transparent in stating that he knew nothing about BPMs and allowed me to continue working the way I had without undue interference. His self-proclaimed role was to connect us with the right people at the client end and 'leave the experts (that was us!) to do their job'. This worked very well, and our then CEO, Raman Roy, often quoted our working relationship as an example of what collaboration should look like!

When you listen to people interfacing with their client, you can really have your finger on the pulse of what is working and what is not. Internally, within the organization, the responsibility of fostering such relationship and collaboration falls on the leaders at all levels.

Exceptional Client Service Makes a Difference

When writing this book, I was asked how vital client management should be for new leaders. And while much of what I have said in this chapter answers that question, I would like to answer it in two words—*absolutely critical!*

I believe that if all things are equal—i.e., if your product or service is at par with the best in the market and your people and pricing keep pace with other players—the relationship between the service provider and the client becomes a key differentiator. While our work does speak for itself, good relationships allow people to *see it* more readily, which builds trust and credibility and can help expand the business. Think about it, if you have three cafés at about the same distance from your home, which charges about the same, wouldn't you frequent the one where people took the time to be more sociable and build a relationship with you? Would you travel a little further and maybe even pay a little more to get to the same coffee? How does this apply to your relationship-building approach with clients?

Strong and Deep Relationships Matter

Story #24

One of the most impactful learning around this came when I had a leading surgeon in Delhi as a client. Dr Anil Khetarpal was and continues to be a great relationship builder. As a pharmaceutical sales executive, I would spend time understanding his business and its challenges. This would give me material to research, and when I felt I had something substantial to offer, I would go back to him and share what I had learnt.

Remember, this was the time when the Internet or Google access was not available. I had to request our marketing team in Mumbai and our headquarters in the UK to fax me relevant articles from various medical journals and research papers. Dr Khetarpal obviously saw some value in what I was bringing because he would stretch his packed schedule to find time to meet with me. We have even had five-minute meetings outside the operations theatre before the start of surgery, and I have shared many car rides with him just for the opportunity to meet and talk! I would even write handwritten letters containing follow-ups, and if I could not meet him, I would leave a note with the secretary. Through these interactions, I was able to build a solid connection and expand the business. A few years ago, we spent a short time together fondly reminiscing over experiences almost two decades old at a chance meeting at the Pune airport.

An equally special relationship that I cherish to date is with another surgeon, Dr Narin Sehgal. He would challenge me to think beyond and would always motivate me to take up new opportunities. His advice and recommendations helped me take a tremendous career trajectory when I switched to the ITeS industry in 1998. I owe it to him and many more clients who have become good friends over these years.

If I were to put in one sentence the gist of what these experiences have taught me, it would be this—never think short term in relationship building. If you are authentic and committed, the benefits are multifold—professionally and personally.

When You Have to Hit 'Restart'/'Reboot'

When I get stuck, I would say to myself, 'Go back to the basics'. Where did the client's expectations diverge from my understanding? Were there unspoken expectations I may have missed out on clarifying and addressing? Usually, these are embedded in the:

- Client organization standards and culture
- Industry standards and quality benchmarks that set the bar for you
- Your personal reputation and that of your organization
- Clear and confirmed articulation of what is expected

I read an article where the author(s) had very cleverly depicted the 15 most 'difficult' clients through illustrations.[72] I find the images of challenging clients in this article quite refreshing on many levels. It is done without being disrespectful and invites us to approach a subject that usually can be incredibly stressful, especially for a new leader, with a touch of humour. Such an approach itself can often take us into a problem-solving mindset that allows fresh energy to flow. A sincere acknowledgement of

---

[72]'15 Types of Difficult Clients and How to Handle Them,' *Digital Synopsis*, https://digitalsynopsis.com/advertising/how-to-handle-types-of-clients-guide/, accessed 30 June 2021.

an oversight or a mistake followed by an action plan can help assuage heartburns and help move forward.

Like in any relationship, when stuck, go back, look for what went wrong, ask questions and discover where new alignments can be created.

Diving Deep: Research Insights

In his book, *All for One*, Andrew Sobel speaks about the DART model for identifying experience co-creation opportunities[73] DART stands for Dialogue, Access, Risk and Transparency. It forces you to think about opportunities to enhance the client experience in each of these areas, as follows:

Lack of Dialogue: What interactions with your client are incredibly one-sided, preventing them from engaging in a conversation with you that might uncover new value? A better alternative, which increases dialogue, is to structure a working session with lots of 'give and take' around the key issues the client wants to solve—a session in which you actually role-model what it would be like to work together.

---

[73]Sobel, Andrew, *All for One: 10 Strategies for Building Trusted Client Partnerships* (Wiley: 2009).

Lack of Access: What interactions are particularly opaque because the correct information is not accessible to either the service provider or the client? For example, if you are a banker or a lawyer, why not ask to read your client's strategic plan? Why not find out the metrics by which your client will be assessed at the end of the year? Why not share an early draft of a report with your client, rather than trying to polish and perfect it for the 'big presentation'? These are simple ways of increasing information flows and access. In my discussion with Sam Swaminathan, he encourages us to do thorough research on the client's business and its impact on the client's customers. Once your client sees the 'trusted adviser' in you, it changes everything.

Lack of Risk Understanding: In what interactions is there a risk, on both sides, that the other side does not understand? In what businesses would a more open sharing of information result in a better distribution of risk? For example, necessary financial disclosure to a company's auditors would enhance their understanding of hitherto opaque risk. Similarly, a technology services firm could make risk more transparent and distributed by sharing information more openly about possible software development delays.

Lack of Transparency: What interactions are incredibly opaque, mysterious or one-sided? Would sharing more information reveal new opportunities? For example, a service provider could involve the client more closely in the staffing of a project, particularly at the project-management level, to ensure a better fit of experience and personalities.

In their book, *Client First*, authors Joseph and JoAnn Callaway reveal how honesty, competence and compassion can become the keys to great success in an organization by creating strong and trusting relationships with clients.[74]

---

[74]Callaway, Joseph and JoAnn Callaway, *Client First: The Two Word Miracle* (Wiley: 2012).

Sometimes, our perception of clients can be that they want to be 'treated like kings' and feel compelled to 'do their bidding'. But if we can create a shift in this frame and remove the implicit sense of control and power, we realize that clients are people, and if we make an effort to connect, build a rapport and understand their needs, then they don't need 'managing' but 'connection'. What needs 'managing' is the relationship; people need connection. This subtle but significant shift has informed my approach to working with clients today.

My client experiences improved based on mutual trust and also because of my increased awareness that the clients, particularly from the western world, like to do straight talk and hate over commitments or incorrect pictures being painted to cover the real issues.

'Yes, I made a mistake, and this is my plan to rectify and recover', is the kind of statement that is more acceptable to clients than being defensive on fundamental issues. Also, it is imperative to make investments in building strong connections. Investments in understanding the client business through reading about them and interacting with them regularly go a long way. Connecting offline to exchange notes on personal interests and hobbies, sharing responsibilities in case of any personal emergencies or otherwise, taking additional work in case of emergency, disaster, extreme weather or technical outage at the client site and more can go a long way. Meaningful dialogues on improving output, recommendations on process improvements, and the sharing of new ideas and best practice are things that clients appreciate. These actions are perceived as those of a trustworthy partner and a trusted adviser.

More than sharing an honest picture and being open to your vulnerabilities, how you plan to address the issue is valued most by clients.

LeaRNiNG

NUGGeTS

To woo a retailing giant, during their visit to the Infosys campus in Pune, the sales and operations team at Infosys collaborated in delivering something unusual. They recreated a typical store to provide a real-life experience on various customer touchpoints, wherein the Infosys software and operations processes could improve the retail giant's customer experience and profitability.

This was well received and highly appreciated by this prospective customer.

While at Cognizant, we had created a village fair setting for a healthcare client in one of our office terraces. This fair had several stalls with people providing information on how they go about client management, how they source a deal, manage the account, why their transition method is better than the competitors and more. This was done using fun themes such as a kaleidoscope, dart game, throw a ring, rifle-balloon shooting, food stalls, etc.

The 3M Story: Welding and not a Wedding!

Sam Swaminathan shared this nugget with me recently. Sam would always try to dig deeper to better understand client needs before embarking on any consulting initiatives. Sam asked his team to coordinate a meeting with top clients who contributed 60 per cent to 3M's business in this endeavour. Sam and his team spent time coordinating and seeking insights on what went well and how 3M's identified business improved its earnings.

This meeting also helped Sam understand the client's plan for the new year. This commitment to go the extra mile helped him forge a deeper bond with 3M—a bond of a trusted advisor. In Sam's words, such relationships become welding and not a wedding!

Delightful Experience at Marriott

Story #25

One of my most memorable customer delight experiences was at one of the Marriott hotels in Nashville, US, many years ago. I had checked out of the hotel and was planning to organize a cab for my airport travel. I decided to grab something to eat as the airport ride was almost an hour long. At this restaurant near the hotel lobby, I was warmly greeted by a staff member. While I was walking around to check out the nicely spread buffet, she noticed a huge smile on my face, triggered by a display of freshly plucked strawberries. It had reminded me of my son, who loved the fruit.

The lady made a quick enquiry if everything was fine, and I made a casual remark about my son's love for strawberries and the fact that this wasn't a strawberry season back in India. Our brief conversation ended, and I went back to my table. As I was heading out, I heard a polite voice, 'Excuse me, sir.' I saw the lady with a large and neatly perforated and packed Thermocol/ Styrofoam cup full of strawberries! She mentioned, 'These are for your son, with love from Marriott. I noticed you are travelling and hence, suggest placing this in the cabin baggage, I am sure they will stay fresh when they reach your son.'

I was touched by this gesture. Every time I walk into a Marriott hotel during my global travels or am invited for a customer service session, I fondly remember and never get tired of sharing this incredible experience of customer delight with my audience! How many of us never miss an opportunity to delight our client or internal customers?

During my visit to Tokyo (in December 2017), I felt slightly embarrassed to see a female employee stepping out of the hotel, helping me load my luggage into a cab, even opening the door and finally bidding me goodbye! While I felt slightly embarrassed to see a lady lifting my luggage and open the door of the car, it was a warm and personalized gesture. It was as if my relative or a friend has stepped out of her house and was saying goodbye to me.

Be open to the bigger vision, challenges put up by your clients. Work backwards to figure out ways to meet this vision.

—Gopal Devanahalli, CEO,
Manipal Education Americas

♦

Your focus on 'care and share' helps build trust. Transparency, sharing of best practices and learning from each other help connect with the client and build stronger bonds. Pour your heart into serving your clients.

—Sam Swaminathan, Senior consultant and storyteller

For You to Reflect in Your Own Light

What key messages have stayed with you from the chapter?

_____

_____

_____

_____

_____

_____

How is your current relationship with your client? What would you like to change in this relationship? What is not serving you? What is going well?

_____

_____

_____

_____

_____

Some of your problems with the clients are like icebergs. You can see a little bit of it, but the part that's hidden from view is more significant and dangerous. The challenge is icebergs can seem like minor problems. Perhaps the tip of the iceberg is an unusual complaint. It's easy to write it off as a fluke or a one-time occurrence. But what if it's just the first sign of a much bigger problem?

Customer service experience author, Jeff Toister suggests making a list of unusual complaints or problems. These don't necessarily have to be the most common customer complaints. Answer the following questions for each situation:

1. Is it possible the same problem has happened before?
2. How likely is it that this problem will happen again?
3. Can similar issues exist in other places?
4. Who else might be affected by the problem?
5. What can we learn from this problem that can be applied to other issues?

_____

_____

_____

_____

_____

_____

Do you feel confident in your communication skills? If not, how can you improve?

_____

_____

_____

_____

Are you enthusiastic about connecting with people and building relationships? What might stop you? And what would you like to do about it?

_____

_____

_____

_____

BUILDING CLIENT RELATIONSHIPS

INVEST
IN UNDERSTANDING the CLIENT'S CORE VALUES AND BUSINESS

CLIENTS appreciate WHEN THEY BELIEVE THAT YOU ALWAYS KEEP THEIR INTERESTS IN MIND

FIND YOUR FEET
Be COMFORTABLE WITH YOUR CULTURAL AND PERSONAL ID

BUILD & NURTURE
YOUR TRUST & GOODWILL

FOLLOW UP
AND CATCH UP WITH YOUR CLIENTS REGULARLY

BUILDING RELATIONSHIPS FROM THE HEART

KNOW the PEOPLE!

COMMUNICATION

VERBAL & NONVERBAL

CLEAR WAY of COMMUNICATION

TRYING to UNDERSTAND OTHERS PERSPECTIVES

REFLECTING ON YOUR ACTIONS

8

DEVELOPING CULTURAL INTELLIGENCE

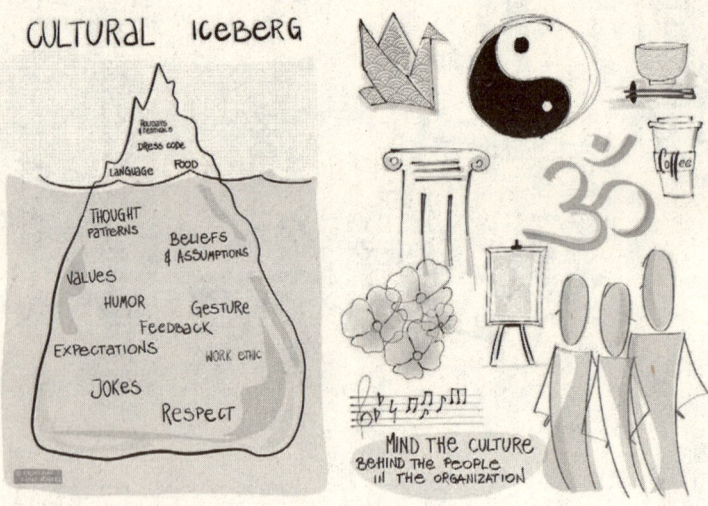

CULTURAL ICEBERG

RELIGIOUS & TRADITIONS
DRESS CODE
LANGUAGE FOOD

THOUGHT
PATTERNS
BELIEFS
& ASSUMPTIONS
VALUES
HUMOR
GESTURE
FEEDBACK
EXPECTATIONS
WORK ETHIC
JOKES
RESPECT

MIND THE CULTURE
BEHIND THE PEOPLE
IN THE ORGANIZATION

Relationships are at the heart of a successful business. Whether you are working with other employees, your boss, company executives or customers, it is their sense of you that matters most. Do they trust you? Do they want to work with you? Are they as committed to you as you are to them? Are truth and honesty the bond that ties you together?

Business is not all black and white. There are different shades of grey too. Having the correct shared principles will guide you in dealing with others. Clear articulation of shared principles become the foundation of a culture where people from different backgrounds and experiences can work together in harmony for the common good.

What I Learnt

> *Set patterns, incapable of adaptability, of pliability, only offer a better cage. Truth is outside of all patterns.*
>
> —Bruce Lee, Martial art expert[75]

One might wonder what Bruce Lee's words have to do with working across and within cultures. In a globalized world, our touchpoints with other cultures have increased exponentially, and with it, the chances of more in-depth understanding and significant misunderstandings. Often, we work with such conviction in our own beliefs, thoughts and practices that the very idea that something completely different or even diametrically opposite might be worth considering, can seem preposterous. Such rigid thinking and working styles can become the proverbial 'cage' that Lee talks about in the quote above. Patterns help navigate daily life, but truth changes from moment to moment and puts it 'outside of all patterns'.

If we do not understand or engage with other cultures, our misunderstanding can lead to a big financial impact. Earlier in this book, I have shared how I managed a situation with a culturally insensitive British client who made inappropriate and unnecessary remarks around India's Independence Day. Throughout my career, there have been numerous such experiences that needed delicate and deft handling. In fact, Mrinalini shares an experience from the early days of her career. While handling the transition of a British insurance process, she and a colleague were responsible for

---

[75]Lee, Bruce, *Tao of Jeet Kune Do* (Ohara Publications: 1975).

communicating the importance of buying insurance to customers. This segment was relatively new in India, and people did not fully relate to the value of purchasing insurance. The duo developed a simulation, which followed an uninsured family's difficulties due to the demise of their primary breadwinner. The simulation was well designed, and a test run was done with the clients to ensure they were on board with the Indian training partners' approach. Needless to say, there was a stark contrast between the Indian and British approach to talking about the loss of a family member. Growing up with our mythologies and religious outlooks, we are far more comfortable talking about life and death than the British. The clients found it deeply disturbing, and the simulation had to be aborted midway.

In the above scenario, a sincere apology and an explanation of why such a simulation was necessary for the Indian context were enough to smooth things out. But faux pas can come in many different shapes and sizes.

Addressing Unspoken Concerns

Story #26

I remember my first trip to the US from GE in 1998, with a team of four colleagues. I was so new to everything that I missed many of the necessary cues needed to build and nurture relationships. The BPM industry was just taking off, and there were many concerns amongst the American workforce regarding the offshoring of jobs and the possible loss of employment for them. This was a sensitive environment to work in. In hindsight, I realized that my presence could have served to address such apprehensions and pave the way for smooth working relationships. Being new to the industry, arena and country, we, the Indian contingent, instead ended up cooking and eating meals separately. The main reason for doing this was our long-duration project of three months. Getting a meal of our choice and that too at a reasonable price was a tough ask. Access to local Indian grocery stores was limited and expensive at the time.

Mealtime in any culture is usually a time and space where people are relaxed and engage in casual non-work-related conversation, hence a great place to build and deepen relationships. I did not pick up on the opportunity, and it was a loss for us. While this does not look like a cultural faux pas, the lost opportunity to explain why we were there and address their unspoken concerns with care left a lot of room for misunderstandings and miscommunications to occur later.

Sometimes, an act of omission can be as significant as an act of commission! Luckily, our visit and subsequent interactions were not marked by any such happenings, yet, my ignorance and inaction left a lot to chance. Interestingly, I learnt a lot from *what I did not do* and now make a concerted effort to clue into concerns, questions and thoughts that may be going unexpressed amongst the people and the team I am working with.

What Is Culture?

The stories that I have shared this far are different in terms of the time, place and culture they are set in. Yet, there is a common thread that runs through all of them—the invisible, yet powerful, force we find ourselves rubbing up against is what we broadly call 'culture'. But what is this ambiguous yet omnipresent beast? And why do we struggle with it as much as we do?

Often, when we think of culture, we think of a country's culture or a large group of people. However, groups, organizations, families and even individuals will have aspects that form their *own* culture and aspects that they share with a larger whole. Yet, defining what exactly we mean by culture can be tricky at times. In school, I often saw culture as clothing, food, rituals and routines of a group of people. Yet, culture is more extensive in its scope and definition and profoundly impacts how we think, feel and relate to each other.

Organizational culture defines a jointly shared description of an organization from within. The same can be said for national or individual culture as well as that of a group or family. While subcultures may exist, the dominant narrative is often understood as the 'culture' of those people. It's a subset of many things that make company culture. The way you recruit, connect with clients/employees and run your business, and frame policies and procedures form the culture of an organization. A good work culture is open, honest, courageous, connected to the customer, and has vast swathes of passionate and engaged employees—this is the kind of culture that enables companies to react and respond effectively to fast-changing markets and environments.[76]

Cultural Intelligence

Cultural intelligence refers to the skill to relate and work effectively in culturally diverse situations. It's the capability to cross boundaries and prosper in multiple cultures. People with high cultural intelligence are attuned to people's values, beliefs, attitudes and body language from different cultures.

Understanding the Context: Key to Leading Well in a Diverse Workplace

According to Sam Swaminathan, understanding context is crucial when dealing with diverse cultures. For example, in the Belgian culture, hierarchy and decentralization work, while in Dutch culture, the opposite works. One cannot apply a broad brush while dealing with this subject of understanding the context of

---

[76]Elliott, Glenn and Debra Corey, *Build It: The Rebel Playbook for World-class Employee Engagement* (Wiley: 2018).

the geography you are operating in. Sam continues to elaborate this with his own example, where one of his sons has married an American lady while the other has married a Brazilian national. He experiences diversity at the core, especially with his grandchildren, who study in an American school with several Chinese, Taiwanese and Portuguese cultures represented in their classrooms! Clearly, these children will have a unique context to cultural nuances as they grow up and connect with the more extensive, professional network.

Sam continues by stating that leaders need to make a conscious effort to find out more about the culture and background of the associates they are dealing with. The understanding must appeal to both the head and the heart.

So, how does one 'tame' or at least befriend this beast called culture when it shifts and changes shape from person to person and from context to context? Getting comfortable with clients from different countries and ethnicities, and organizations take a certain amount of preparation, patience and humility. Being aware of your own possible biases and prejudices vis-à-vis the other is also helpful. Often, being unaware of our own understanding of our culture and the other is the first stumbling block. Familiarizing yourself with your own prejudices, biases, opinions and proclivities can be seen as the first step in the process of getting savvy in building cross-cultural relationships.

Culture is a dynamic body that evolves over time and shifts from moment to moment. We cannot have one way to address the cultural nuances. Culture is ever evolving and dynamic. Since we can never fully understand culture—ours or another's—our openness and curiosity are more critical than harried attempts to learn all relevant holidays and foods of a particular culture. Spend time in cultivating a healthy curiosity to identify, understand and appreciate the clients' cultural nuances as well as those of key stakeholders.

Being sensitive and careful and having the willingness and drive to learn are essential. Working successfully across cultures means not expecting a smooth, wrinkle-free ride; *au contraire*, it is our capacity to get comfortable with newness, strangeness and uncertain outcomes that help us engage different cultures better. To once again borrow the words of Bruce Lee, 'Be water, my friend.'[77] Water takes on the shape of the vessel that holds it without losing its essence. That is what constitutes 'water-I-ness'. This ability sets the stage for successful engagement across cultures. In the various organizations where I have worked, there have been different methods by which we picked up on the cultural nuances of clients and other key stakeholders. At Glaxo, it was often through observations and informal learning that we learnt to navigate these spaces. Also, there was too much bureaucracy at play which gave a somewhat biased view around culture. At GE, it was through more formal channels and through hands-on experience at client sites in different countries. At Infosys, my learning has been through a combination of formal training and informal education during visits to the US, the UK, China, Latin America, Mexico and South East Asian countries.

Personally, I find hands-on learning in cultural contexts extremely helpful, though preparation and inquiry provide a great starting point. Astute observation and keeping an open mind pave the way for successful intercultural exchanges.

Additionally, building a good network of people who will reflect back to you is extremely helpful. We sometimes have a blind spot where our own openness is concerned, and getting insights from others who know us well and whom we trust, can be a blessing. I have been lucky enough to have very open-minded and supportive clients and colleagues who have been instrumental in helping me recognize my drawbacks and strengths in this area.

---

[77]Lee, Shannon, *Be Water, My Friend: The True Teachings of Bruce Lee* (Rider: 2020).

Also, inputs from seniors and peers who had more experience in dealing with different nationalities or had long stints on foreign shores were immensely helpful.

Cultural Balance Begins with Awareness

Even though the business world works along professional lines, sometimes there are unspoken 'hierarchies' and biases that show up without stepping into socio-economic and political spaces. Navigating our way through new and often unfamiliar cultures can be a delicate issue. Managing business relationships and associated impact on the bottom line tend to add to the pressure. In such situations, I find that it is OK to lose a battle to win the war, but where the line is crossed, take help from seniors and escalate the matter. It takes a certain amount of reflection and maturity to gauge the right way to respond in such situations. It helps me when I am mindful of not stepping into areas that can be incredibly explosive; in organizational exchanges, it's essential to stick to business concerns because it may not be *necessary* to bring every identity to every space. If there is discrimination, bias, etc., it is essential to bring it up.

If there are cultural hierarchies at play and those seep into work relations, they can upset the dynamics and impact productivity. Here again, it helps to clarify your own feelings and reservations about your culture and that of the other. If there is something that makes us uncomfortable, making peace with who you are and where you come from provides the confidence to interact with people without inadequacy. Even a particular brand of jingoism can indicate discomfort with another's cultural identity. Neither over-adapting nor overcompensating helps in building healthy work relations. Behaviours that help build a better cultural alignment with a client or colleague from a different region or country include:

- Making attempts to help the client understand and appreciate better aspects of our culture while simultaneously looking for some parallels that can be drawn.

- Being proud of your culture and drawing attention to its positive side while being realistic. There are positives and negatives everywhere. It is good to introspect how you feel about your culture and country and be grounded in that when you travel for work.

- Assessing the client's hesitations and gaining confidence might require working around fears, apprehensions or a naive understanding of your culture.

- Taking the available opportunities to reach out and talk about your country and culture as you experience it. On one of my visits to the US, I remember speaking with an eighth-grade geography class at the behest of a client's husband. He was a teacher there and thought it would be a good idea for the students to learn about India from someone who lives here. This was not in my job description, of course, but it was an excellent way to build bridges, professionally and culturally.

- Another incident that stands out for me was one from early 2015, when I carried little tokens for my American counterparts. I brought an idol of Lord Ganesha. We ended up having a brief conversation on the management lessons we can learn from Ganesha. The big ears tell us to listen more and well. The large stomach represents an enormous appetite for learning and growth. This was an unexpected treat that came out of a simple gesture of courtesy.

Learn the Idioms

Story #27

We surely need to strike a balance and know what action is required in different circumstances. There is no fun in winning an argument and losing a customer, and often I find many issues are a simple case of crossed lines of communication. I remember, while managing a UK-based telecom major in 2006, I was taking a break and saw some of my clients heading home for the day, and the client said, 'It's been a rough week, and we are going uphill now.' After the weekend, I asked how their visit to the hills was. They laughed and said it was an old British idiom that meant retiring for the day and heading back home. Since we have a lovely hill station close to where I live in Pune, my assumption on the clients visiting the hill station had its own reasons.

On his next visit to India, the client vendor-manager brought me a British idioms book, and I appreciated the gesture instead of being offended. The ability to laugh at yourself and accept you made a mistake with authenticity is essential. Sometimes, we can go into a shell and try to defend our point of view without an absolute requirement for it, which is not helpful. Styles of humour differ from culture to culture, and there is no harm in seeking clarification; in fact, it enhances our understanding of the other.

With some of my sporting clients who have become great friends, I have been playful in introducing them to unique and spicy Indian dishes such as paan (beetle leaves) and jal jeera (a tangy and spicy local drink). Not everyone can sign up for such gastronomic adventures! However, robust bursts of laughter over food and drinks make it a worthwhile attempt.

When we try to understand the demographic and show our interest in people and their culture, they often respond with openness. Whenever in doubt, it helps to politely enquire. Asking someone to bring a friend or a partner to dinner is acceptable if it is done politely; even refusing to eat something offered is fine as long as it's phrased well. Saying, 'You've been so gracious, and I hope it doesn't offend you, but I don't eat seafood,' is infinitely better than a blunt 'no' without preamble. Most large organizations have a diversity office that takes care of training, sensitization, etc.

It might be a good idea to reach out to them and get their inputs. However, nothing teaches you better than first-hand experiences.

Breaking of Protocol Happens

Story #28

I remember my first experiences with people being laid off. It was in 1998, when the words 'lay off' and 'rightsourcing' were relatively new. Today, most of us know what they mean. I was with GE, and several people were being let go of in our offices in the US. I would notice a poster at the cafeteria's entrance with a daily countdown of the number of days left, along with a picture of one of the employees being laid off. While my team and I did not quite understand the implications, as we bumped into this gentleman in the cafeteria, we empathized in our own Indian way by saying things like, 'I'm so sorry for your loss.' The gentleman replied matter-of-factly, 'That's how life is!'

There was something about how he said it, which made me think that perhaps we had overstepped somehow. Though I will never know how he received the news, on reflection, it occurred to me that our offshore company was contributing to his experience in one way. The culturally appropriate thing would have been to not raise the subject with him. Our sincere statement could easily have been misinterpreted as adding insult to injury.

So, was this the first or the only time I tripped up in my career? Far from it! There have been many instances when inadvertently, a protocol gets broken and a line crossed. In my years in the corporate space, I have developed several ways to manage such slip-ups, and I am happy to share them here:

- Assess to see if the responsibility for the situation lies with you. Most often, we must carry at least *part* of the burden simply because, in human interactions, both people are responsible for the outcome.

- Apologize promptly. If you have a good and open relationship with the person or client, seek inputs on how things could have been better.
- Once you have figured out what the lapse was, make sure you rectify it and take care not to repeat.
- Plan ahead for meetings and interactions that are likely to require a deeper cultural understanding of the other side.
- Ask questions and create checklists on what to do and what to avoid when engaging with people from various cultures.
- Check to see if you can ascertain the preferences and expectations of the individuals with whom you are to interact.
- When in doubt, clarify and seek the help of seniors or other people who have experience in the demographic you are engaging with.

After the GE experience, we attended transition communication sessions run by the project champion, which helped us to understand these sensitive contexts better and develop the language to appropriately address the issues, when required. So, whether we learn about varying cultures through formal training or through hands-on experience, acquiring knowledge and having an open attitude are essential. Walking into situations with a willingness to engage and understand serves a leader well in her journey through her career.

Gopal Devanahalli recommends that one generally be curious and interested to explore, learn more about your client's culture, and leverage it socially and from a business perspective. He says lack of cultural sensitivity and understanding can become a barrier to the success of your business.

These days, it's widespread to see businesses in the tech industry export some or all of their development work to other countries where the labour costs are much lower than what they would be in the US or in Europe. These kinds of circumstances call for constant collaboration between American and European onshore teams and their offshore counterparts. Generally, when companies scout countries to outsource their work to, they might consider, among many others, the following factors: i) time zone; ii) human capital and iii) ease of travel.

But what about the cultural compatibility between one country and another? What about the way Americans conduct meetings in their country? In comparison to it, how would a meeting be organized in Latin America, India or China? Does their small talk last longer before they put pen to paper? Or do they have a similar 'let's-get-to-the-point' approach, like in the US?

If we are going to live with our deepest differences, then we must learn about one another.

—Deborah J. Levine, Author

When working in a cross-cultural context, all parties involved must make an effort to understand one another to get the most out of every interaction we have with our teammates. Having a cultural understanding between yourself and your foreign counterparts allows for a more accurate expectation to be set regarding productivity and the overall commitment to the tasks at hand.

If you calibrate with a team from Latin America, you may have to learn to accept that it's common for people to take at least an hour for lunch or even step out of office for two and a half hours to run an errand. If you have got people in your team from China, you will have to learn to negotiate and do business with them based on the importance of group representation.

Whatever the case may be, pay attention to the cultural nuances and take them into consideration. It could be the difference between more business and better results for you and your team or slow and stagnant progress because you cannot seem to see eye to eye with the group of individuals from across the pond. No matter where a person is from, they will always prefer to work with someone relatable.

Technology is making the world move faster, making competition fiercer. Companies are innovating and changing at a rate previously unimagined. Product life cycles are shorter, links between manufacturing and the customer are closer, and the demands for process improvement and process change have never been greater. We have never needed our staff on our side more than we do now. Just look at the time taken for new products to reach 50 million users. The radio was invented at the start of the twentieth century, and it took 38 years to get 50 million listeners, but 100 years later, it took just four years for the iPod to reach the same sized audience. It took only three years for the Internet, a year for Facebook and a month for Angry Birds!

Would it not be interesting to know the exact time it would take the TikTok app to reach 800 million users worldwide? This speed generally makes better outcomes for the customer, but it also brings enormous instability. With technology, new players with small, highly engaged teams can outmanoeuvre and outperform their larger, slower competitors. Look what happened to Nokia, Polaroid, Blockbuster (video rental chain in the US) and Borders (bookstores in the US). These companies failed because when the winds changed, they could not move fast enough, reorganize themselves quickly enough or stay connected to the customer closely enough. You could say they all failed because of the failure of their corporate cultures. Great cultures are full of openness, honesty, courage, connection to the customer, and vast swathes of passionate and engaged employees—these are the cultures that enable companies to react and respond to fast-changing markets and fast-changing environments.

Diving Deep: Research Insights

Twenty-first-century organizations need culturally intelligent managers and leaders. The pressure to build authentic global networks and cultivate an appreciation and respect for cultural differences and similarities have driven cultural intelligence to the forefront of diversity and inclusion work.

My research took me to interesting models shared by Mai Moua (CEO, president and consultant at Leadership Paradigms, Inc.)[78], and David Livermore (author and expert, Cultural intelligence) in his book *Leading with Cultural Intelligence: The Real Secret to Success*[79].

Cultural Intelligence Model

Cultural intelligence is a framework to help you learn to turn off your 'cruise control'. Like a computer that has been on for too long, is overworked or has multiple programmes running

---

[78]You may want to refer to this link to make a deep dive and explore the work of Mai Mua at: https://open.umn.edu/opentextbooks/textbooks/136, accessed 1 July 2021.

[79]Livermore, David, *Leading with Cultural Intelligence: The Real Secret to Success* (AMACOM: 2015).

simultaneously, which caused it to freeze/hang, we have to learn to reset our mental programming. Sometimes, resetting it once or twice does not work; you will need to turn it off completely by taking a pause and then returning to it at a later time.

Cultural intelligence emphasizes three areas: metacognition and cognition, motivation and behaviour. Metacognition and cognition represent your ability to think, learn and strategize. In cultural intelligence, the principle of motivation refers to your self-efficacy and confidence, your ability to be persistent and the alignment to your personal values. Behaviour, in cultural intelligence, is about your ability to have a repertoire of skills and your ability to adapt your behaviour.

The framework for cultural intelligence consists of the following parts: knowledge, strategic thinking, motivation and behaviours. It may be helpful to think of these as the ABCDs of cultural intelligence: **A**cquire, **B**uild, **C**ontemplate and **D**o.

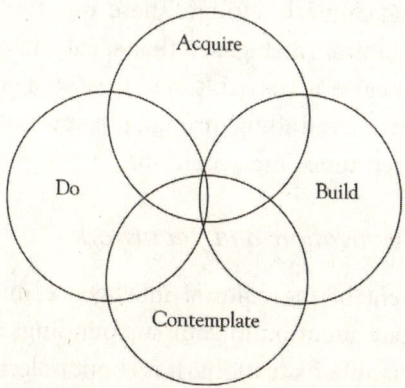

Figure 8.1: Cultural Intelligence Model

Acquire Knowledge

A fundamental piece of inter- and cross-cultural interactions is the knowledge a leader has when working with cultures unfamiliar and different from his or her own. Knowledge is a central tenet in intercultural training and is included in the cultural intelligence model because it is essential for any person, whether leading or managing, to be attentive to cultural systems. You must know how cultures are created, interpreted and shared, as well as how cultural interpretations, meaning and symbols can impact behaviours and attitudes.

You can think about this aspect of the model as *acquire* because you need to acquire information and knowledge that help you identify cultural elements at play. The acquisition of knowledge—i.e., tapping into what you have stored in your memory—is cognition.

Build Strategic Thinking

Once you gain knowledge about the culture, how will you use it? What parts of the knowledge obtained will you use? Will they all fit, given the cultural setting? These questions address the component of cultural intelligence that speaks to your ability, as a leader, to strategize across cultures. It is your ability to *build* awareness of your surrounding through preparation and planning. It is often referred to as 'metacognition'.

Contemplate Motivation and Teamwork

The third element of the cultural intelligence model speaks to your ability to pay attention to your surroundings as well as your responses to unfamiliar situations. It is about reflecting upon your own interests, your drive and your motivation, as well as your willingness to work through and with cultural interactions.

You can think of this component as *contemplate* because it requires you to be present—to take a step back, suspend your judgments and biases, reflect upon your assumptions and listen carefully. It requires that you be alert and remain aware of your cultural surroundings. As a leader, presence allows you to identify the cultural scripts that are hidden and to recognize when to turn them off.

Adapt and Perform

Richard Carlson, a noted author, said that 'everything we do has the potential to influence another human being... The key element here is not to second-guess yourself but rather to become conscious of how your life choices influence those around you'.[80] In one of his books, Carlson speaks of our level of conscious choice in day-to-day living.[81] When do we choose to adapt to our environments? Because of a choice we made, what did we let go? How has our choice affected our beliefs and values?

These questions address the fourth component of cultural intelligence, which is your adaptability and ability to perform new behaviours based on new cultural surroundings. Are you aware of how others see you and how you come across to them? How do you interpret what others say, and how do you respond? Culturally intelligent leaders are like chameleons in social environments, changing their behaviours to mimic their surroundings.

David Livermore, one of the foremost experts on cultural intelligence, provides compelling reasons to embrace cultural diversity. According to him, contemporary leaders encounter dozens of different cultures daily. It's impossible to master all the norms and values of each culture, but effective leadership does require some adaptation in approach and strategy. Executives identify cultural intelligence to be crucial, considering the following pressing issues:

---

[80] Cited in *Leading with Cultural Intelligence,* Page 69, https://www.opentextbooks. org.hk/system/files/export/27/27507/pdf/Leading_with_Cultural_ Intelligence_27507.pdf, accessed 11 July 2021.
[81] Ibid.

- Diverse markets
- Multicultural workforce
- Attracting and retaining top talent
- Profitability and cost savings

In fact, 90 per cent of leading executives from 68 countries identified cross-cultural leadership as the top management challenge for the next century.[82]

The model recommended by Livermore focuses on four capabilities of a culturally intelligent leader. These are:

- Drive
- Knowledge
- Strategy
- Action

Drive is your level of interest and energy to adapt cross-culturally. Do you have the confidence and drive to work through the challenges and conflicts that inevitably accompany cross-cultural assignment?

Knowledge is the cognitive dimension that refers to your understanding of culture and its role in shaping how business is done. Do you understand the way culture shapes people's thinking and behaviour?

Strategy, also known as the metacognitive dimension, is your ability to strategize when crossing cultures. Can you slow down long enough to carefully observe what's going on inside your mind and the minds of others?

Action, the behavioural dimension of CQ[83], is your ability

---

[82]Livermore, David, *Leading with Cultural Intelligence*, Chapter 1, Page 13 (American Management Association: 2015) https://davidlivermore.com/wp-content/uploads/2015/02/Chapter-1_Leading-with-CQ_Livermore.pdf, accessed 11 July 2021.

[83]CQ is an abbreviation used for 'cultural intelligence/cultural quotient'. It can be understood as the capability to relate and work effectively across cultures,

to *act* appropriately in a range of cross-cultural situations. Can you effectively accomplish your performance goals in different cultural situations?

Starbucks's Chinese Tea Houses

When thinking about being culturally intelligent as leaders, Starbucks's love affair with China comes to mind. Its first store in China opened in 1999 and looked like a traditional Chinese tea house. It was a big success and currently operates an estimated 4,000 stores in China. How has this mega-company succeeded in a country which traditionally favours drinking tea? With a growing number of Chinese middle-class people purchasing high-end goods and western technologies like laptops, portable music players and smartphones, Starbucks has smartly decided to interact with its customers through marketing that have 'Chinese

---

bearing similarity to the term 'cultural agility'. Originally, the term 'cultural intelligence' and the abbreviation 'CQ' was developed by the research done by Christopher Earley (2002) and Earley and Soon Ang (2003).

characteristics'. In 2015, the coffee company also partnered with Alibaba, a Chinese company similar to Amazon, to launch an e-commerce site.

However, Starbucks's relationship with China has not always been without bumps. In 2007, a store located in the Forbidden City, a nearly 500-year-old palace and a designated United Nations World Heritage Site, was closed. The reason for this closure was an Internet campaign started by Rui Chenggang, a TV anchor, who stated on his blog that the store 'tramples over Chinese culture'.[84] The American coffee shop was then replaced by a Chinese coffee shop called The Forbidden City Café.

Starbucks understands that the world is more interconnected than ever. Tailored Internet marketing campaigns and the traditional look of Chinese stores show how the company thinks of Chinese consumers as an individual, rather than a mass market. Together with the positive way its employees are treated, these strategies create a solid foundation necessary for Starbucks to expand in China.[85]

Culturally intelligent leaders can adapt when working in multicultural contexts. Some of the questions to ask are:

- Is it a 'tight' or 'loose' culture?
- Will adapting compromise the organization or me?
- Will retaining the differences make us stronger?

---

[84]'Debate Brewing over Forbidden City Starbucks', NBC News, 19 January 2007, https://www.nbcnews.com/id/wbna16692792, accessed 1 July 2021.
[85]Butch, Taylor, 'How Does Starbucks Succeed in China?' The Diplomat, 4 July 2016, https://thediplomat.com/2016/07/how-does-starbucks-succeed-in-china/, accessed 1 July 2021.

Over the years, I have come to understand that culture isn't just one aspect of the game. It is the game—the only competitive advantage. The crucial part is actually building the team that will embody the company culture and propel it forward. If you get your culture right, paramount aspects such as great customer service, building a great long-term brand or empowering passionate employees and customers will happen on its own.

Clifford M. Pai, VP, H.R. Head. APAC & EMEA
and Global Head–Employee Relations, Infosys BPM

◆

Culture impacts organizational success and influences execution. It connects people and performance.

—Rakesh Malhotra, President and CEO,
Global Natural Resources Inc.

Water the flowers and they will grow strong. Water the weeds and they engulf the flowers. Leaders hold the watering can and will get the garden they choose to water.

—Bobby Chatterjee, Senior Director, HR, Hertz

For You to Reflect in Your Own Light

What key messages have stayed with you from the chapter?

_____

_____

_____

_____

_____

Think of your own prejudices, biases, opinions and tendencies about a particular culture (could be of your client's country or of your own team). Observe, look up or ask your trusted resources from that culture for information that challenges your existing belief system.

In the column on the left-hand side, write down the initials of six to 10 people you trust the most. But remember, they should not be family members.

Name	Gender	Nationality	Native Language	Accent	Race/ Ethnicity	Religion	Professional Background

Now, place a tick beside those members of your trusted circle who are similar in gender, nationality, native language, accent, age, race/ethnicity, professional background and religion. For example, if you are a male, you will place a tick beside all men in your trusted six. You will discover that your trusted six often display minimal diversity—for most of us, our inner circle includes people with backgrounds/cultures similar to ours.

Consider the implications of this for the workplace? For example, as leaders, when you do not expand your worldview and are not open to having people from diverse cultures in your circle, how well do you think your cultural intelligence will thrive?

CULTURE

STAY CURIOUS

UNDERSTANDING

Context IS CRUCIAL WHEN DEALING WITH DIVERSE CULTURES

WHAT HAPPENS WHEN YOU TRIP UP?

CLARIFY
¿??¿

SORRY

APOLOGIZE PROMPTLY

CHECK IF YOU CAN ASCERTAIN the PREFERENCES & EXPECTATIONS

CREATE CHECKLISTS ON WHAT to DO AND WHAT to AVOID

WATER the FLOWERS and they WILL GROW STRONG. LEADERS HOLD the WATERING CAN and WILL get the GARDEN they CHOOSE to WATER.

GREAT CULTURES ARE FULL OF :

OPENNESS

Honesty

courage

CONNECTION

to the CUSTOMER

Be WATER, MY FRIEND.

Bruce Lee

© 2023 NILUN TASIA IBRAHIM

and the need to keep learning is more important than ever.

The thirst for learning new approaches, new techniques, new solutions and new ways of empowering followers, further risk-taking, and sharing of new ideas, problems and successes—these make a leader.

Learning from a Mentor

Story #29

I was seven years old when I lost my father. With my sister married and my brother out of the country, I spent a quiet childhood, keeping to myself, making my way through year after year of education without feeling inspired. Much later, I was able to see that I am a hands-on learner who needs to *do* things in order to learn. Engaging in activities and immersing myself in experiences is how I have learnt and grown in my life and my career. Unfortunately, most schools in India do not provide that opportunity, or at least that was the case in my school at that time.

School years were not an incredibly engaging time for me, and without encouragement from teachers, I found myself unmotivated and a little adrift. However, with a few teachers' support, I got more involved in the last few years of school and college. Without an early academic inclination or the financial support required for a professional degree, I worked where I could pay bills and sustain my family and myself. Having done well in college as a Botany and Zoology graduate, I was lucky to find myself working for a pharmaceuticals company even before I received my graduate degree; this was the beginning of a challenging, eventful and eventually, fulfilling career and life.

While I would have loved to go through formal management education, the years ahead showed me that as long as I am willing to engage with my environment openly and learn what it has

9

BE A LEARNER AND A LEADER, FOR L

'The curious mind will stay relevant.' This is what I believe ir
say often. Learning is forever. It does not stop when you get o
school. It does not stop when you complete the onboard trai
for your new job. It does not stop when you change jobs. If
are gifted with life itself, you will feel the need to keep learr

Learning is behind every outstanding achievement—f
learning how to make a fire to explorations to Mars to plan
intra-planet travel. The world continues to change faster and fa

to offer, I will move forward in life. I figured out early on the importance of constant learning. As explained in the earlier chapter on the need to have mentors and its benefits, I found that my next-door neighbour, Mrs Chandra was my Google, Alexa and Siri of the '80s! Her library of resources (i.e., magazines and books) and her time provided the much-needed cerebral nourishment. Like Siri and Alexa, she too would help fuel my curiosity, provide quick answers to many unsolved questions, correct my pronunciation, teach me table manners, introduce me to global music and more. Long conversations with her over tea and coffee helped me overcome my self-limiting beliefs. I owe a lot to her in grooming me ahead of my corporate life.

'Constant Learning' has been further enriched by what has been coined 'Learnability'. It must be familiar to all employees working at Infosys and many large IT firms. It is a phrase coined by Narayana Murthy[86] and subsequently popularized by the former CEO of Infosys, Vishal Sikka. It can best be defined as an ability to learn and adapt to new situations or the ability to observe and understand the rules of a continually changing game and excel at it. At Infosys, 'learnability' is often defined as 'the ability to extract generic inferences from specific instances and using them in new, unstructured situations'.

For me, it is eventually about the need to stay relevant to whatever you are doing. This truth comes back to me very often as I move through the world—whether while watching kathak performers integrate western drums into their repertoire or seeing how several new brands of phones are racing ahead of the iPhone and Samsung. Things are moving forward at a rapid pace, and the faster we can learn and unlearn, the quicker we move with it.

---

[86]When asked why he was building the Mysore campus, he explained it was to create a workforce with the 'propensity to learn'.

The Slope of Learning

Story #30

As a young professional, my learning curve had to be steep. When I moved from Agra to Delhi to work with Glaxo Pharmaceuticals (now GSK), the game changed drastically. Luckily, I had a manager who focused on the fundamentals and suggested I have my own business suit to wear when I meet the senior executive for my final interview. He also recommended me to brush up on my reading on Human Anatomy. Unfortunately, I did not have a business suit and instead borrowed a loose-fitted one from my uncle. Concerning reading, I got a recommendation from my cousin to procure second-hand books sold on the pavements near a famous theatre in Old Delhi. I picked up a few books relevant for the interview, and comfortable to my pocket.

We had to check the prescription habits, whether they were recommending our medicines or not and if anything else was required. Keeping up to date with the doctors and hospitals in our sales territory was a crucial part of our job. That day, I forgot to carry my folder containing notes and the Glaxo MSL (Must See List), which was essentially a list of consultants and doctors we had to meet and follow-up on. The manager sent me back home to get it. The painful two-hour trek home and back to the meeting place impressed upon me the necessity to keep on top of the basics. Perhaps, the review could have been done without it, but the output quality would not have been the same. Now I make it a point to carry a notebook or a digital pad to review meetings and discussions.

Instances such as this can quickly become anecdotes of a rough or annoying day, or they can impress upon us the need to focus on the fundamentals and learn.

Learning from a Colleague

Story #31

Sometimes, a colleague's experiences can prove to be just as valuable as our own. One of the sales executives at Glaxo was having a tough time setting up a meeting with a senior doctor. One day, as luck would have it, he saw the doctor pull out his car; he decided to hide his scooter and requested a ride with the doctor instead. My colleague's quick thinking and presence of mind were rewarded. He was able to connect with the doctor at a deeper level due his undivided attention as they drove through the streets of Delhi for about an hour! As they became friends, he was later able to share with the doctor how he had nailed that fortuitous meeting with him.

In today's changing world and business environment, there is so much information available to us that we begin to believe that learning can only happen in one way. What is marvellous about cultivating a curiosity around learning is that we do not have to *know* everything; we just have to know how and where to find wisdom when we need it.

The Competitive Advantage of Learning

As a Glaxo pharmaceutical sales executive, I dealt with specialized high-end products. Convincing a doctor to prescribe a cancer treatment support medicine that costs ₹400 ($10/tablet) in 1995 meant I had to know what I was talking about. My innate hunger to learn came in very handy here. I used to get details from medical journals available only in the UK via Telex. This was to build my case as to why these medicines were better than our competitors, such as Lily-Ranbaxy, Hoechst and Cipla. While my job description did not specify that I had to learn every minutest detail on the molecules behind the drug, going that extra mile gave me an advantage when discussing side effects and impact with a doctor. In the absence of the Internet, journals and reference books such as *The Lancet* and *Monthly Index of Medical Specialties* came quite handy.

Besides this, Glaxo made continued investments in our learning. I recall spending time at the cancer wards of the Tata Memorial Hospital in Mumbai. The visit was anchored by a senior oncologist, who explained the dreaded disease's details and made us meet a few patients undergoing cancer therapy. His aim was to help us understand the after-effects of chemotherapy and radiotherapy so that we could relate better to the pain the patients were going through. This, in turn, improved our discussions with oncologists during our sales visits.

Another instance where I saw value in developing my inclination towards learning was, when I was a GE employee and had travelled to Orlando, Florida, in 1998. We were transitioning a project for the newly created GE Healthcare in India, and I was to spend three months learning all I could about the business in the US. The early years of globalization were an exciting time, and we could not take for granted many of the things we have today, such as fast typing speeds and easy laptop access.

At the end of an intense workday, I arrived at my desk to see a box with Typing-Tutor software had been left on my desk by the project leader, Gary. He had seen my team and I struggle with typing. Those days, as the manager, I was the only one who was given a laptop, and he saw that we were unable to transition and document the processes as rapidly as was required. The gesture could have been poorly received. However, I saw the value in what was being said, and I set up a roster at home with others in my team to take turns improving our typing skills.

As recent as May 2017, I completed an eight-week programme on Inspiring Leadership from Case Western University via Coursera (a learning programme distribution platform). Not only was the programme interesting, it further opened my thinking on Emotional Intelligence, the subject of focus in the programme. After completing this programme, I got rewarded by being offered an opportunity to curate a learning programme on emotional intelligence for a large UK-based bank. One of the reasons they selected me was the credentials around the content, faculty and the university. Swaminathan's (Swami) message around 'earning follows learning' once again came alive through this experience.

As the COVID-19 pandemic has triggered the work-from-home culture, almost everyone has realized the need to be digital-ready and proficient depending on the job, role or business. Zoom meetings and several webinar platforms such as Cisco's Webex and Google Meet have seen their popularity soar. Everyone from young students to homemakers, doctors, teachers, yoga gurus and the elderly have quickly transitioned to digital learning. YouTubers and vloggers have become gainfully busy. Journalists have been learning technical skills to produce, edit, market and broadcast their content from their living rooms.

As a leadership facilitator and coach, I have been investing in various masterclasses to hone my virtual learning skills. Along with several like-minded professionals, I recently signed up for a course to explore the world of digital learning. This helped in making my offerings more engaging and impactful using various methods and techniques. Investments in buying studio equipment to record, broadcast learning events and conduct live sessions for my clients and student community have been beneficial.

After completing our masterclasses, a few of us have created a 'virtual warriors' group on WhatsApp to share learning and seek support. Our regular meetings over Zoom practising several tools, sharing new applications and conducting mock digital learning sessions have taken care of the initial hesitation. We have now become comfortable with various programme design and delivery processes, including new-age software and hardware tools.

With the recent initiation of Curious Learning Circles[87] in my city, many professionals from diverse backgrounds attend a book reading session followed by discussions on learning and application. This learning circle has become even more famous through its digital avatar during the lockdown period.

I invite you to reflect, create or join similar learning circles in your city to help you expand your horizons beyond your day job. Learning from adjacencies helps improve your skills. Sourav Ganguly, another celebrated cricketer and former captain of the Indian team, practised football to improve his cricketing skills. He transitioned from a traditional five-day test match to a game of 50 and 20 overs, called One Day International (ODI) and T20, respectively. Being an aggressive sport, playing football requires tremendous stamina, agility and aggressiveness to produce results in flat 90 minutes. Saurav's investment in learning football added an extra punch to his performance and helped India win several tournaments, including the coveted World Cup title.

Improving the Curiosity Quotient

The steady movement from intelligence quotient to emotional quotient and now to curiosity quotient (CQ)[88] has necessitated that we learn intensively from the environment while being selective and knowing what to focus on to achieve our unique goals. Fostering a healthy appetite for learning is essential.[89] Identifying

---

[87]This is an informal meeting scheduled every fortnight where the trainers/facilitators connect via Zoom platform to enhance their learning. We get a guest speaker to share their experiences and also share latest updates on virtual learning methods.

[88]Friedman, Thomas L., *The World Is Flat: A Brief History of the Twenty-first Century* (Farrar, Straus and Giroux: 2005).

[89]Chammorro-Premuzic, Tomas, 'Curiosity is as important as intelligence,' *Harvard Business Review*, 27 August 2014, https://hbr.org/2014/08/curiosity-is-as-important-as-intelligence?autocomplete=true, accessed 1 July 2021.

what you can bring to the mix will keep you relevant and nurturing that with focused learning will help you grow. Feed your curiosity and experience the positive change it brings to your life.

I chose to move from a relatively conservative pharma sales to the sales training industry and subsequently to the ITeS world, which opened new learning opportunities. In my view, the best part of being a part of the BPM/ITeS world is being able to experience multiple clients, verticals and industry domains within one organization.

I began my US healthcare journey from GE in 1998 and moved to tech support operations for a global giant in 2000, followed by supporting one of the largest credit card organizations across multiple geographies in 2004 and leading operations for a large UK insurance and a telecom giant in 2006. This was followed by an opportunity to lead and serve the customer services domain until 2010. This role allowed me to serve 13 clients from different industries (i.e., telecom, manufacturing, banking, digital, media and more).

Finally, until 2016, my role as Training Head provided an immersive experience in developing capabilities to serve the business process requirements of more than 150 clients across the globe. Of course, this meant getting out of one's comfort zone, many years of night shifts, extensive travels, training and certifications. An old proverb proved right for me as much—'no pain; no gain'.

When leaders cultivate curiosity, the impact can be felt in their lives and those of their team members. Therefore,

- Develop curiosity to become better leaders. Be curious to learn more about their domain, the client pain areas and their teams.
- Learn what 'good' looks like and share best practices with others. Continue to improvise and share your learnings with others.

- Develop or learn why team members struggle with new skills. Learn new skills or enhance existing ones to help teams better.
- Develop curiosity about their own and their customer's businesses. A deep understanding of organizational goals and client goals and requirements go a long way.

A well-known fable tells us that, if a frog is put suddenly into boiling water, it will jump out, but if the frog is put in lukewarm water, which is then brought to a slow boil, the frog will not perceive the danger and be cooked to death.

While scientifically, this story is not valid, it aptly demonstrates what can happen if we ignore the ever-evolving changes in the environment. In the current climate of artificial intelligence, blockchain and BOT-driven process automation, if we do not unlearn and learn new skills and get cross-skilled with more unique ways of learning, we will become redundant.

The top skills that will be needed by 2025[90] are:

- Analytical thinking and innovation
- Active learning and learning strategies
- Complex problem-solving
- Critical thinking and analysis
- Creativity, originality and initiative
- Leadership and social influence
- Technology design and programming
- Technology use, monitoring and control
- Resilience, stress tolerance and flexibility
- Reasoning, problem-solving and ideation

How many of these skills were relevant about a decade ago?

---

[90]'The Future of Jobs Report 2020,' *World Economic Forum*, 20 October 2020, https://www.weforum.org/reports/the-future-of-jobs-report-2020/in-full/ infographics-e4e69e4de7, accessed 11 July 2021.

According to estimates from Statistica (a research website), the number of smartphone users was 2.5 billion in 2016 and 3 billion in 2018 and is growing so fast that it has already crossed 6 billion people in 2021.[91] This exponential growth in information access has changed the landscape of all industries and sectors.

The pandemic has further triggered the need for higher levels of empathy and emotional intelligence. Learning new skills, deepening your current skills and openness to the ever-changing environment have become the need of the hour. Work from home, relocation to one's hometown and hybrid work environments have added to the challenges. Please note, not everyone has the desired space, tech infrastructure or comfort to work from home.

Despite this massive sea change in the way people connect, an ex-colleague and a senior executive told me that the digital explosion was irrelevant to his business as a large share of his business is conducted through traditional channels. Now, that is a frog about to be boiled!

Keeping Pace with the Digital Revolution

To add to this digital revolution, the popularity of wearable technology and devices such as Fitbit, Amazon Echo, Google home, etc., are clearly progressing towards a more extensive and pervasive connection with customers. Organizations and executives who are in the denial mode will be left behind by the organizations leveraging this opportunity to enhance their work areas' customer experiences. The current pandemic has further reinforced the need to be more agile, trusting and practising empathy-driven leadership skills. Such skills would be equally relevant beyond 2021.

---

[91]"Number of smartphone subscriptions worldwide from 2016 to 2026," https://www.statista.com/statistics/330695/number-of-smartphone-users-worldwide/, accessed 11 July 2021.

In his article for the World Economic Forum in 2019, Stephane Kasriel, CEO of Upwork (a popular freelancing website), mentions:[92]

- Artificial Intelligence and robotics will ultimately create more work, not less. Much like the case today.
- There will not be a shortage of jobs; however, if we do not take proper steps, there will be a lack of skilled talent to fill those jobs.
- As remote work becomes the norm, cities will enter the talent wars of the future. Untethering work from the place will give people new geographic freedom to live where they want, and cities and metropolitan regions will compete to attract this new mobile labour force. (We have already experienced work from home, gig working, and more unique opportunities in the wellness space, telemedicine and psychiatric space).
- The majority of the workforce in the US will freelance by 2027, based on workforce growth rates found in this study.[93]
- Technological change will keep changing at a rapid pace, so learning new skills will be an ongoing necessity throughout life.

The COVID-19 pandemic has only affirmed Kasriel's predictions. Quite a few organizations are building 'Hybrid Models' that include a certain percentage of employees working from home and small offices in the heart of the city.

---

[92]Kasriel, Stephane, 'What the next 20 years will mean for jobs—and how to prepare,' *World Economic Forum*, 10 May 2019, https://www.weforum.org/agenda/2019/01/jobs-of-next-20-years-how-to-prepare/, accessed 11 July 2021, [93]'Freelancing in America,' *Upwork*, https://www.upwork.com/i/freelancing-in-america/2017/, accessed 2 July 2021.

Diving Deep: Research Insights

Always consider yourself in permanent beta, i.e. as a work in progress, eager to learn and develop.

—Reid Hoffman, LinkedIn and PayPal co-founder

◆

Learned individuals make learned organizations. Organizations learn only through individuals who learn. Individual learning does not guarantee organizational learning. But without it, no organizational learning occurs.[94]

—Peter M. Senge, Author

With learnability being such a necessary trait to cultivate, I have often wondered what makes it difficult for people to learn. I believe any leader who hopes to create a culture of learning needs to be familiar with the *process of learning* and the possible setbacks an individual might face. Being able to place where the person is on the Competence Curve (see image) can be a significant step in successfully moving through all the learning stages.

---

[94]Senge, Peter M., *The Fifth Discipline: The Art and Practice of the Learning* (Deckle Edge: 2006).

When Swaminathan, my leader at Infosys BPM, said that people avoid learning when they have gaps they feel they can't bridge, he refers to the *process* of learning. Sometimes, a gap in learning can create a distaste for the subject or an aversion to learning new things altogether. He often spoke of how people find escapes when they have negative experiences. One can only imagine how damaging that can be for an organization's health—to have a workforce that is either unwilling or unable to learn. The process of understanding learning needs is essential if we are to create an employee-driven culture of learning and growth within organizations.

Competence Curve

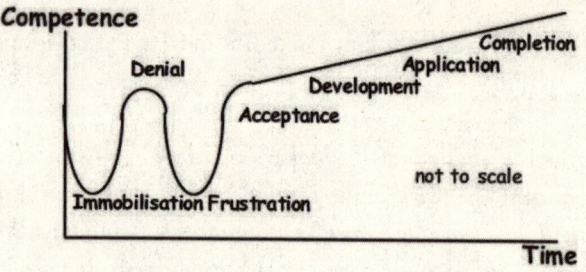

Source: Hay, Julie, *Transactional Analysis for Trainers* (Sherwood Publishing: 2009).

The Competence Curve was a concept introduced by Julie Hay, who practises a psychology method known as 'Transactional Analysis'. Through her diagram, she illustrated how the normal learning process has two points at which a learner may give up. The first is the stage of immobilization frustration, which usually occurs when the learner is faced with a requirement to learn something new or change. And the second is when the learner has overcome the initial resistance, but faces disappointments and frustration after the first attempts have been made. The capacity to identify which stage the learner is at will provide critical guidance to a leader in deciding whether, when and how to intervene. In her books, Hay talks about the importance of a role model, mentor or a helping hand at the frustration stage. The presence or absence of one can determine the outcome of the learning process.

So, while organizations champion the idea of a learning culture, they must ensure that they provide the tools and techniques to create it and to *think* about it. Our objective should be to help enhance the learnability quotient and cultivate that in employees. Expecting frustration and setting up systems and processes to create timely and appropriate interventions will allow employees to move through the stages to completion, giving them the confidence to tackle more learning initiatives. Understanding the learning process lets us plan for the frustration and anxiety that can accompany learning. By understanding and appreciating the learning process, we can preempt the possible roadblocks and plan our strategies accordingly.

The Individual Styles of Learning

Another aspect of how we learn has to do with individual preferences and inclinations. Taking the time to know your learning style can be valuable in aiding your learning processes. Would you learn better by shadowing a leader, listening to podcasts or watching videos and presentations? This differs from person to person, and being familiar with your own style will allow you to access information in formats that facilitate learning. Mrinalini is primarily a visual learner, and images stay firmly with her. I am a visual and experiential learner. Today, books and workshops are not the only way to learn. Information is available through a range of channels, and it is up to us to know and decide what works best for us.

I have been a restless leader and learner, always seeking opportunities to learn and grow from the context I was in. Trying new things, experimenting and, at times, failing have been the hallmarks of my career. If young leaders were to take one single thought away from this book, it would be this—if life presents an opportunity to do the proper management course, then do it, but if for some reason, you are unable to do so, I recommend exploring short-term online courses offered by Coursera, LinkedIn Learning, Udemy, etc. Subscribe to leadership magazines and forums. Contribute and seek help from your network. Read, observe, keep the interest going and you will learn, and as long as you keep learning, you will grow. And that is at the centre of good leadership.[95]

The Discomfort of Learning

Story #32

Sometimes, seeds sown through one or two experiences can shape significant aspects of our life. Even negative experiences can drive us to excel and outdo ourself. I remember trying to learn to swim at the Army pool in Agra as a child and being put off by some of my classmates when they held my head down in the water as a prank. Later, as a 25-year-old, when I tried learning again, I needed a medical certificate, and the doctor laughed at my enthusiasm to 'learn swimming at *this* age!' I persevered and luckily found a coach, albeit, a much younger one and half my size!

Seeing me standing closer to the shallow end of an Olympic-size pool, nervous, he asked me to trust him, which I did, a bit reluctantly though. He ordered me to jump into the pool and I followed his advice. Now, I swim to exercise, relax and remind myself that there isn't anything that we can't learn if we want it bad enough, focus on it and keep looking till we find the support

---

[95]Peter Senge's book *The Fifth Discipline: The Art & Practice of the Learning Organization* (Currency: 2006) can have a tremendous influence on how we understand learning within organizations and the impact of interventions. I recommend this book to everyone who wants to understand how to improve their learnability.

we seek to get us to the other side. The only commitment you must make is the willingness to lean into information, to accept the discomfort of learning new requirements and accept a new way of viewing your work landscape.

Albert Einstein said, 'The measure of intelligence is the ability to change.'

Learning Half-life

A few years ago, I got introduced to an interesting concept of *learning half-life*. Until a few years ago, the learning half-life was around 10 years. This would mean that whatever you learnt 10 years ago, almost half of it would be relevant today. Any guess what would be the learning half-life in the current context? Well, it is for 13 months! It means whatever you have learnt over the last 12–13 months, only half of that new knowledge is relevant in the current context. Do I need to provide more reasons to encourage people to make learning one of their most critical agendas?

Reinvention and relevance in the twenty-first century draw on our ability to adjust our way of thinking, learning, doing and being. Leaders must get comfortable with living in a state of continually *becoming* a perpetual beta mode. Leaders who stay on top of society's changes do so by being receptive and able to learn. When the half-life of any skill is shrinking, leaders bear a responsibility to renew their perspective to secure their organizations' relevance.

Personal Knowledge Mastery (PKM)

I find the term Personal Knowledge Mastery (PKM) coined by Kenneth Mikkelsen and Harold Jarche quite fascinating.[96] According to these authors, sustainable competitive advantage depends

---

[96] Mikkelsen, Kenneth and Harold Jarche, 'Leaders Are Constant Learners,' *Harvard Business Review*, 16 October 2015, https://hbr.org/2015/10/the-best-leaders-are-constant-learners, accessed 2 July 2021.

on having people who know how to build relationships, seek information, make sense of observations and share ideas through intelligent use of new technologies. To help leaders do that, the authors developed the PKM process, a lifelong learning strategy. It is a method for individuals to control their professional development through a continuous seeking, sensing/making and sharing process.

Seeking is about exploring and keeping up to date. In a world overflowing with information, we need intelligent filters to sort out valuable information. It requires that we regularly evaluate and adjust the information sources we base our thinking and decision-making on. Today's matters are connected to a wise network of trusted individuals who can help us filter helpful information, expose blind spots and open our eyes.

Sensing/making is how we personalize information and use it. Sensing includes reflection and putting into practice what we learn. It is a process based on critical thinking where we weave together our thoughts, experiences, impressions and feelings to make meaning of them. By writing a blog post or noting down ideas, we contextualize and reinforce our learning.

Sharing includes exchanging resources, ideas and experiences with our networks and collaborating with our colleagues. Sharing is a contributing process where we pass our knowledge forward, work alongside others, go through iterations and collectively learn from important insights and reflections. We build respect and trust by being relevant when we share with our social networks or speak in front of a crowd.

There is a wide range of digital tools out there for each of the PKM activities that can be fitted into a busy schedule and help people become self-directed, autonomous learners. Which tools to use depends mainly on the context and personal preferences. Tools are essential, but mastery in the digital age is only achieved if you know how to establish trust, respect and relevance in human networks.

By seeking, sensing and sharing, everyone in an organization can become part of a learning organism, listen to different frequencies, scan the horizon, recognize patterns and make better decisions on an informed basis.[97]

Finally, we live in a world of *overwhelming information/ abundance of information*, so sieving out the relevant information is becoming a new challenge.

Hence, the need to access *contextually curated content* is of utmost importance.

Nelson Mandela's 'ndiwelimilambo enamengamo'

A beautiful example of life-long and life-wide learning that I would like to mention here is that of Nelson Mandela. Mandela's autobiography, *Long Walk to Freedom*, is written almost like a learning story.[98] It is a tribute to his teachers. He dedicates it to his teachers, his learning and all that has shaped him.

---

[97]Mikkelsen, Kenneth and Harold Jarche, 'Leaders Are Constant Learners,' *Harvard Business Review*, 16 October 2015, https://hbr.org/2015/10/the-best-leaders-are-constant-learners, accessed 2 July 2021.
[98]Mandela, Nelson, *Long Walk to Freedom* (Abacus: 1995).

Another example of his exemplary learning spirit is his use of the Xhosa[99] phrase, '*ndiwelimilambo enamengamo,*' which means 'crossing famous rivers'. Mandela used it when he returned from Johannesburg to the Eastern Cape for the funeral of a chief. He realized how he had changed in that journey, how he had moved from a rural area to the city, how he had become an urban person, a lawyer, from being a Thembu, a tribal person. One thing that is characteristic of Mandela is this ability to reflect on what is going on around him and understand what it means. He not only learned throughout his life but also became an example of life-wide learning. The learning was not just confined to formal spaces like schools and universities but included prison, the struggles— it was an 'embracing learning'. To him, life-deep learning was not merely about politics and law but also about how a person grows and develops. Mandela's writings are an extraordinarily rich reservoir of material about life-long learning.

Kiran Mazumdar-Shaw: Accidental Entrepreneur

Kiran Mazumdar-Shaw might be one of the richest self-made businesswoman in India, but she calls herself an 'accidental entrepreneur'. She is the founding chairperson of the Indian biopharmaceutical company, Biocon. She was taught by her brewmaster father to respect anyone who works hard at doing a good job. She relies on her husband to keep her grounded. 'He always reminds me of a critical saying: people that mind, don't matter, and people that matter, don't mind.'[100] Simply put, relying on others is how she leads. 'I am like a sponge. I absorb a lot.

---

[99]A member of a South African people traditionally living in the province of Eastern Cape.

[100]BW Online Bureau, 'A Legacy of Leadership,' *BW Businessworld*, 8 November 2014, http://www.businessworld.in/article/A-Legacy-Of-Leadership/ 08-11-2014-69722/, accessed 11 July 2021.

I like to hire people who are smarter than me,' she says, adding there are two styles of leadership. 'There are leaders who want to command and control. The other kind of leader focuses on collaboration and empowering people. I like to do the latter.'

I loved what she said in one of the interviews for Your Story[101]. She says,

> It's a voyage of discovery, you basically learn how to deal with the problems, you learn how to solve problems, you learn how to deal with business issues, with regulatory issues, all these things are very alien to you when you get into building a business. Then you realize there is a formal process. It is not just doing something in an ad hoc way. There is a rationale for what you must do. There is a strategy to what you do, and so you slowly, sort of, learn on the job.

[101]Sharma, Shradha, 'The unstoppable walk of an Indian woman, inspiration and Kiran Mazumdar Shaw,' *YourStory*, 19 November 2014, https://yourstory.com/2014/11/kiran-mazumdar-shaw, accessed 2 July 2021.

Be perpetually optimistic and a life-long learner.

—A.K.N Prasad, Avionics expert and former head of
Management Development Programs at Welinkgars
(We Business School, Bangalore, India)

◆

*No seed grows a large tree on its own. Soil, water and sunlight
make it happen. Learnability is just the seed.*

—Aman Zaidi, Performance coach,
Storyteller and Facilitator

For You to Reflect in Your Own Light

What key messages have stayed with you from the chapter?

_____

_____

_____

_____

_____

Go on a search for a 'curious learning circle' that makes the most sense to you (in-person or virtual). This could be a coffee club of entrepreneurs or a group of book lovers. Cannot find one? I encourage you to form one in your circle. List the options/ideas here.

_____

_____

_____

_____

_____

Pencil curiosity into your schedule. Set aside 10 minutes every day for intentional curious thought. This might mean tinkering with an old clock or reading an article on a topic you're interested in, just for fun. Jot down a few possibilities here.

_____

_____

_____

_____

_____

Identify someone in your life who exemplifies curiosity. Plan to spend a few hours observing their behaviour and language as if you are with your curiosity role model. Observe their way of being and ask yourself: how can I apply some of their findings to my own attitude of curiosity?

_____

_____

_____

_____

_____

For your next meeting, ask your team to come armed with a piece of inspiration that excites them. Sharing it together can help you find links and patterns that can lead to your design solution. Take notes.

_____

_____

_____

_____

_____

_____

Try adopting a beginner's mindset. Check your own misconceptions, stereotypes and biases, and approach a challenge with fresh pair of eyes. As you work on your own projects, keep asking why and what if—especially when you think you know the answer. Record your reflection.

_____

_____

_____

_____

_____

_____

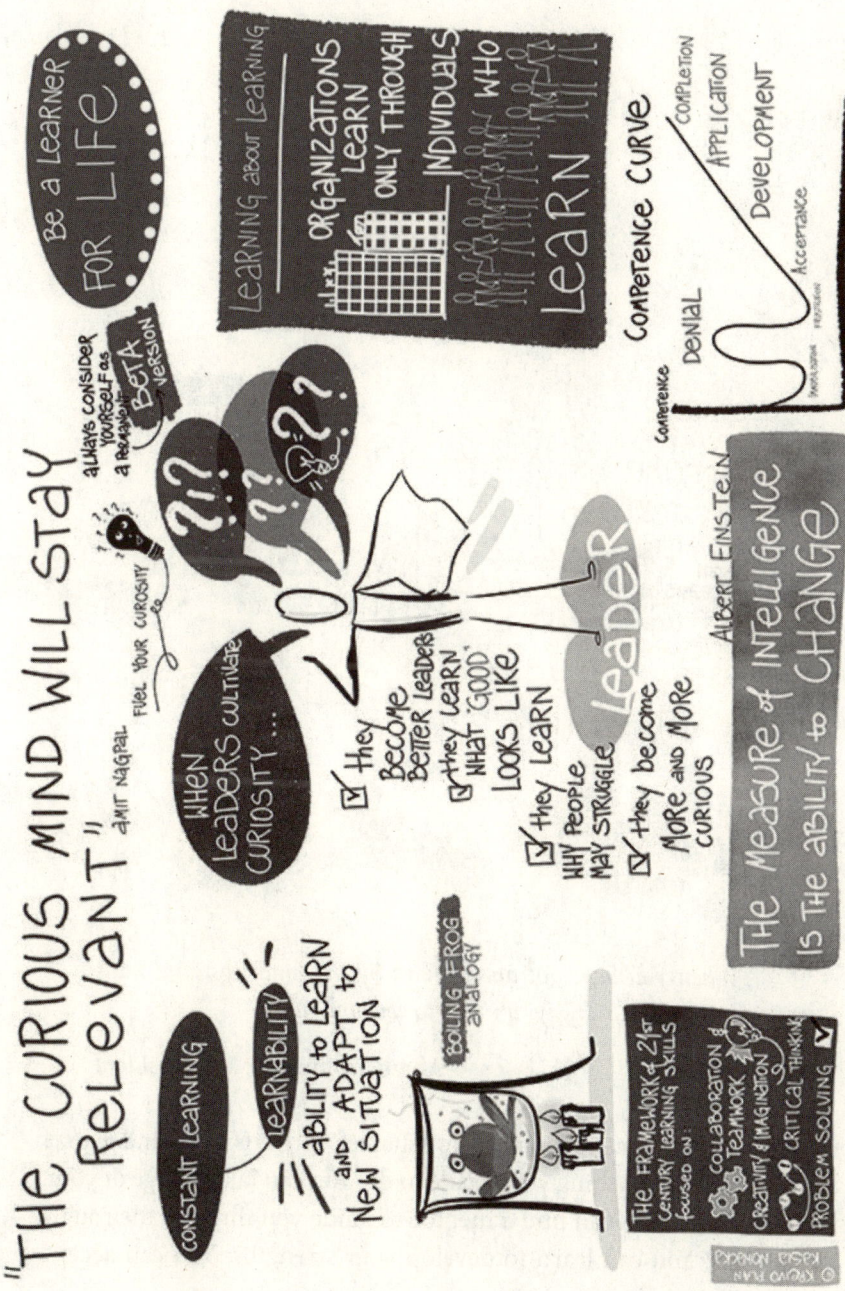

10

SUMMING UP

When you have got an elephant by the hind legs, and he is trying to run away, it's best to let him run.

—Abraham Lincoln, US President

Remember that elephant from Chapter 1? He is a reminder that you can do anything you decide to do. You can take charge of your emotions. You can find a mentor to guide you through the rough waters. You can learn to develop your strengths. You can accept that you will make a few mistakes along the way and that is OK.

You can treat your employees as co-creators and empower them to develop solutions just as good, or even better, than your own. You can gain clients' trust, so they see you as a partner, not a vendor.

You can help mould a new culture in your organization, one that encourages diversity and shared values. And as you learn along the way, you can learn to appreciate learning itself. Become a life-long learner and enjoy the fullness of your potential as the best example and the best leader you can be.

The Beedi Story!

Story #33

As I draw the curtains on this book, here's a story that I heard from Sam Swaminathan during his leadership development session at Infosys a few years ago. This story revolves around the need to stay curious and focus on the why.

One of Sam's relatives, a senior government administrative officer in the south of India, was quite amused to be told that he would have to sign on a register mentioning the number of beedis rolled by his staff that day. It was acceptable to write 'zero or nil rolled' and sign the record. Beedi is the local version of a cigarette made by rolling tobacco over a unique leaf grown in south India. It is cheap, without a filter and provides an instant nicotine kick to people who cannot afford regular cigarettes.

On further investigation, it turned out that one senior officer fancied beedi during the British era. This official started patronizing his new-found love by shipping boxes of freshly rolled beedis to his friends in the UK. To keep track of the numbers, effort and associated fee to the workforce, he had set up the process of maintaining a daily record.

It had been more than 70 years since the British left India, and the senior British officer was long gone, but the process of tracking the number of beedi's rolled continued in this India office until Sam's relative took interest and ordered this to be discontinued. Imagine the amount of stationery, efforts and office space that would have been misused to retain a redundant practice, with no one questioning it for over 70 years!

I have shared many stories and made several recommendations in this book and on my website, https://www.amit-nagpal.com/books/. I would like to draw your attention to the need to question, reflect, challenge the status quo and keep acting basis our experiences.

We all should build a repertoire of exciting and meaningful life stories for our grandkids, nieces, nephews and more! I have boarded my adventure boat and invite you to hop in or identify your own!

Rethinking Leadership: The Way Forward

In my view, the current pandemic is nothing short of a tipping point that has made everyone around the world pause, reflect and take actions to serve and lead in the new normal.

We are experiencing a historical reset, shifts in the geopolitical environment and validations around remote working and work from home. It is not surprising to witness agile organizations responding to this enormous shift and pivoting to newer products and services. For example, in India, Domino's Pizza has tied up with ITC to deliver essential groceries, leveraging its well-oiled pizza delivery operations. Within a record period of 10 days, Asian Paints set up its hand sanitizer product development and launch. Several reporters across the globe have been multitasking, from recording and editing to being involved in the final production of their stories from their homes. The fashion and jewellery industry has swiftly embraced technology for virtual demos, virtual fashion shows and virtual trials using artificial intelligence and phone applications.

We have moved into a state of constant disequilibrium and hence, the need to continue being innovative and always remaining in a state of permanent beta. The new-age leader will have to develop his crisis-management capabilities more than ever.

Leadership is all about influence, and that will never change. In the coming years, impactful leaders would be the ones who offer hope and inspiration through trust and genuine connect, both in person and online. These leaders will have to demonstrate swift actions, decisiveness and empathy. We would need leaders who can guide us through turbulent waters and inspire confidence through this uncertain world's peaks and troughs. The new-age leaders need to bring in an entrepreneurial and learning mindset.

The need to stay curious, the quest for more learning, the building of reliable networks, learning through juniors, peers and subject matter experts and being playful will be crucial for the survival and growth of individuals and businesses. Openness to learning new skills, updating and deep diving in the chosen field will serve well and help us stay relevant.

My journey beyond Infosys since mid-2016 has been nothing less than a roller-coaster ride. This has been a significant move for me. A transition from a structured and a relatively predictable life to a more flexible, independent, purposeful and gratifying life. I found myself boarding the famous Space Mountain adventure machine, a high-speed indoor roller coaster at Disneyland. Despite several years of preparation in anticipation of an independent talent development practice, I experienced quite a few highs and many lows during this five-year entrepreneurial journey.

A business meeting with one of my prospective clients, David Peck, in San Francisco, in September 2016, provided me with a renewed sense of direction and hope. David encouraged me to 'stay committed to myself and honour my dreams', and for that I continue to be grateful.

Since June 2018, after the completion of my Co-Active

Coaching programme and successful work-related visits to Tokyo and San Diego, my goals and the future road map became much clearer.

When I recently stumbled upon old photographs taken during that trip, I saw the beautiful reflection of flowering trees on the sparkling-clear lake at the Emperor's Garden in Tokyo. I quickly googled to find any connection between water and reflection. Typical of Google, within nanoseconds, it invoked a renowned Persian poet, Rumi, who had mentioned this several hundred years ago, and I quote, 'Let the waters settle, you will see stars and moon mirrored in your being.'

These three years (2016–18) were quite unsettling, and it was about time I allowed the waters to settle. I am blessed to have found clarity, a renewed sense of purpose and actions associated with it.

I began work on this book in 2014, with eight themes in mind. To my pleasant surprise, Anneke's research findings reverse validated my selection of the eight themes. I am delighted to share that almost 100 per cent of my clients have hired me to work for them within the realms of these eight chosen areas. This has been a great validation and an encouragement to continue to deepen my learning experiences in these areas.

The elephant at the dinner table is clearly dancing! Let go of his leg and join him!

Resource Bank

I have curated a unique 'Learning Wall' made up of well-researched learning resources aligned to the book's eight themes. Padlet Inc. powers this Learning Wall. You can access this fantastic resource bank 24/7 via a mobile app and website.

Here's a QR code for quick access:

I recommend you sign in to Padlet at www.padlet.com (free access), especially if you want to be notified of my newly uploaded articles and videos and engage with fellow readers and me.

Once you have signed in to your Padlet account, you can join 'The Elephant at the Dinner Table–Learning Wall' by copying the link shared below:
https://bit.ly/3pwSGig

Happy learning!

Amit Nagpal
www.amit-nagpal.com
amit.nagpal@pursuitica.com